BECAUSE WORDS CREATE

Start Speaking Your Power

AUDREY DARIC

To all the women reading this. May this book remind you of your unique worth, your power to create, and the endless possibilities available to you when you believe in yourself.

To my daughter, Hailey, who has inspired me to grow and become the best woman I can be. Being your mom has been one of my greatest blessings, and you are truly my best friend. You have a light that shines bright. Keep shining!

To Amanda and Madeline, my daughters-in-law. I'm so grateful for you and the love you bring into our growing family. I hope these words land gently in your hearts, and know how much you matter.

With so much love,

- Audrey

Passion. Purpose. Power.

They live in you.
Passion is the spark that reminds you life is meant to feel alive.
Purpose grows as you discover who you are and what truly matters to you.
Power is the knowing that you can change, choose differently, and create a life that reflects your values and your truth.
When you believe in your ability to grow, heal, and rise, everything begins to shift.
This is your life.
Step into it.
We can do this.

CONTENTS

INTRODUCTION

Words have a way of staying with us.

You may remember a kind phrase that lifted you on a hard day, or a careless comment that still echoes years later. Words, whether spoken by others or whispered quietly in our own minds, become the background rhythm of our lives. They influence how we see ourselves, how we interpret the world, and how we respond to everything that comes our way.

Take a moment and notice your own inner voice. When life feels heavy, when you're overwhelmed, disappointed, or unsure, how do you speak to yourself? Is that voice supportive and steady, or critical and demanding? Most of us move through our days without realizing how much our emotions, reactions, and choices are shaped by the words running quietly beneath the surface.

Those stories matter. They influence how much we trust ourselves, how we handle relationships, whether we take risks, and how we move through both joy and challenge. Over time, they quietly shape our confidence, our choices, and even the way our bodies respond to stress, fear, or hope.

This is the heart of *Because Words Create.*

This book exists because learning the power of words changed my life in real and lasting ways. I saw how the language I believed, repeated, and lived by shaped my happiness, my relationships, and my sense of what was possible. I learned that when you change your words, you change your inner environment. And when your inner environment changes, your life begins to change with it.

Words teach.
Words influence how you feel.
Words guide your actions.
Words shape belief.
Words create.

Everything in this book is written with intention, care, and deep respect for the woman holding it. My vision is for these pages to feel supportive and grounding, not overwhelming or demanding. A place you can return to when you need clarity, encouragement, or a reminder of who you are becoming. A place that reminds you that your past does not define you, and that no matter where you are right now, you have the power to create something new. A space that helps you see yourself with more compassion and recognize the power you already carry.

Like many women, I've experienced seasons of doubt, comparison, and old stories that made me feel smaller than I truly was. I know what it's like to carry beliefs that quietly limit you. I also know what happens when you begin choosing words that support you instead of tear you down. When I changed the way I spoke to myself, my emotional landscape softened. My confidence grew. My choices shifted. I became more willing to trust myself, try new things, and step into new chapters with hope.

That is why I wrote this book.

Because every woman deserves to feel capable, grounded, and worthy of a meaningful life.

Maybe right now you're carrying doubts, worries, or beliefs that tell you you're not enough. Maybe you've tried affirmations before and felt unsure, awkward, or skeptical. Real change doesn't require perfection, and it doesn't happen all at once. But even small, consistent shifts in the words you use can create powerful momentum. They can calm your nervous system, change your perspective, and help you respond to life with greater clarity and confidence.

Because Words Create is not just a collection of quotes. It is a practical guide to becoming aware of your self-talk, learning how to shift it, and building the daily habit of speaking to yourself with intention. Each chapter offers tools, reflections, affirmations, and rituals designed to support real growth through themes such as determination, motivation, courage, confidence, self-love, forgiveness and gratitude.

This book isn't about pretending everything is positive all the time. It's about awareness and choice. When you become aware of what you're thinking and saying, you reclaim your power. You get to choose whether the words you're carrying support you or hold you back. And that choice changes everything.

As you move through these pages, give yourself permission to pause, reflect, and experiment. Try on new words. Release the old stories that no longer serve you. Speak to yourself the way you would to someone you love deeply. Allow yourself to feel curious, hopeful, and open to what's possible.

My hope for you is simple and heartfelt.

I hope this book brings a sense of calm when your mind feels busy. Peace when things feel uncertain. Hope when you need reassurance. Happiness in small, meaningful moments. And a growing awareness of the abundance already present in your life. I hope these words lighten your heart, brighten your perspective, and remind you—again and again—that you are supported, capable, and creating something beautiful.

CHAPTER 1

THE POWER OF WORDS

"Every thought we think is creating our future."

— LOUISE HAY

There was a time in my life when I didn't realize how much my words were shaping my reality. I wanted happiness. I wanted confidence. I wanted a life that felt lighter and more fulfilling. On the surface, I was learning about positivity, self love, and personal growth. Inside, though, I was quietly resisting the very happiness I said I wanted.

I didn't know it, but I was self sabotaging myself through the way I thought about who I was and what I deserved. What I believed to be true about myself was more powerful than any affirmation I tried to repeat. Deep down, I didn't really believe I deserved to be happy. That was for other people. I wanted it, but I didn't trust it.

Whenever something went wrong, my mind automatically turned inward. It must be me. I must have messed something up, again. That fear of always doing something wrong lived quietly beneath my thoughts and decisions. I didn't question it. I just accepted it as the truth.

When I began to pay attention to my inner dialogue, I started to understand why certain patterns kept repeating in my life. My words were not just describing my experiences. They were shaping how I reacted, what I expected, and what I allowed. I wasn't attracting chaos because I was broken. I was attracting what matched the stories I was telling myself.

This is where the real power of words begins.

Our words are not just sounds or passing thoughts. They become beliefs. Those beliefs influence how we feel. Our feelings guide our actions. And our actions shape the life we experience. Words are the starting point of that entire cycle.

Why Words Matter: The Science of Self-Talk

Our brains latch onto patterns, especially ones we repeat internally. Research from Stanford University, led by psychologist Dr. Carol Dweck, shows that mindset is not fixed. Our beliefs about our abilities and potential directly influence our outcomes. When you repeatedly tell yourself, "I'm stuck," your brain begins searching for evidence to support that belief. But when you shift your self-talk to "I can learn this," your mind opens to new possibilities. This is not about blind positivity. It's about how your daily thoughts shape your behavior, your effort, and your willingness to grow.

Neuroscience supports this in powerful ways. The brain has the ability to change and adapt through a process known as neuroplasticity. Each time you repeat a thought, your brain strengthens the neural pathways connected to it. Over time, familiar thoughts feel more believable and automatic. When your self-talk becomes more supportive, you are not just encouraging yourself emotionally. You are training your brain to respond differently, making growth, confidence, and resilience feel more natural.

The Science of Words and Energy

Every thought, every whispered word, carries energy. Dr. Masaru Emoto, a Japanese researcher, demonstrated this in his water crystal experiments. He exposed water to words, music, and even thoughts, then froze it to observe ice formation. Positive words like "love" and "gratitude" created beautiful, symmetrical crystals, while negative words like "hate" formed disordered, fragmented structures.

Our bodies are about 60 percent water. If the energy of words can influence water, imagine how your thoughts and self talk influence your physical and emotional state. This is a profound reminder. The words you speak to yourself, kind or harsh, matter not just emotionally but physically too. Choosing your words wisely is a step toward shaping your life and your well being.

Your nervous system is constantly listening. It responds to the language you use by either signaling safety or signaling stress. When your self talk is harsh, rushed, or critical, your body often reacts with tension, shallow breathing, or fatigue. When your words are supportive and reassuring, your body softens. Your breath deepens. Your system settles.

This is why words can feel calming or overwhelming almost instantly. They are not just thoughts in your mind. They are messages your body receives and responds to in real time.

Repetition Feels Like Truth

Negative self talk often runs quietly in the background. Statements like "I always mess things up", "I am not enough", " I am unlovable" or "I will never get it right" can feel factual because they have been repeated for so long. But repetition does not equal truth. It only means practice.

When I started learning about self love and positive thinking, I was excited. I thought once I had the right tools, everything would change quickly. What I learned instead was that these are skills. Skills take time. And learning them requires patience, compassion, and commitment to yourself.

There were days I felt discouraged. Days when I wondered if anything was really changing. But even on those days, something was different. I understood myself better. I reacted calmer. The hard moments didn't consume me the way they once did. I was learning how to pause instead of spiral. That alone changed how I experienced life.

Growth doesn't always look like everything is getting better. Sometimes it looks like responding differently. Sometimes it looks like choosing calmer words. Sometimes it looks like meeting yourself with kindness instead of criticism.

Words matter because they teach your nervous system what to expect. They tell your body whether it is safe or under threat. They influence how you show up in relationships. They affect whether you try again or retreat. Over time, they become the foundation of your identity.

Affirmations are one way to begin shifting this foundation. They are not magic statements. They are intentional reminders. When you repeat a supportive phrase consistently, you are giving your mind something new to practice. Over time, that practice becomes familiar. Familiar becomes believable. Believable becomes embodied.

Skepticism is normal. Many people feel awkward using affirmations at first. That does not mean they are not working. It means you are learning something new. Just like physical strength, mental strength is built through repetition.

Words also carry energy. Your thoughts and language influence how you feel physically and emotionally. When your words are harsh, your body tightens. When your words are supportive, your body softens. This connection between words and energy is not abstract. It is experienced every day.

Negative Patterns and Awareness

The first step in changing your life is awareness. Notice the words you use when things feel hard. Notice how you speak to yourself when you make a mistake. Notice what you believe about your worth, your abilities, and your future.

Ask yourself gently:

- What am I telling myself right now?
- Is this helping me grow or keeping me stuck?
- Is there another way to look at this?

Write it down. Seeing your thoughts on paper creates clarity. It helps you recognize patterns that are easy to miss when they stay in your head. Awareness is not judgment. Awareness is progress. Awareness is understanding.

Once you know where you are, you can begin choosing where you want to go.

Ask yourself:

- How do I want to feel in my life?
- What kind of relationship do I want with myself?
- What words would support the person I am becoming?

This is where intention begins. When your words align with how you want to feel, your actions begin to shift naturally. Small steps become easier. Decisions feel clearer. Confidence grows through practice.

Try adding a few love-filled phrases throughout your day:

- "I give myself permission to rest without guilt."
- "I am learning to show up for myself with consistency and care."
- "I create peace through small, intentional choices."
- "I am enough in this moment, exactly as I am."
- "I choose to nourish my body, my mind, and my spirit."

You Hold the Pen

Manifestation is not about wishing. It is about participation. When you change the words you repeat, you change what you notice. When you change what you notice, you change how you act. When you act differently, your life responds.

Everything begins with what you tell yourself. Thoughts shape feelings. Feelings guide actions.

Actions create patterns. Patterns create your life. This chapter is your invitation to become aware. To listen differently. To recognize that your past does not define you. You are not broken. You are learning. And learning means you have the power to choose new words, new responses, and new possibilities.

Your story is still unfolding.

You hold the pen.

You cannot change what you are not aware of. Many of the beliefs that shape our lives are not loud or obvious. They live quietly beneath the surface, influencing how we speak to ourselves, how we make decisions, and how we treat our own needs.

One of the simplest ways to discover your negative story is to listen to your inner dialogue during everyday moments. Pay attention to what you say to yourself when something goes wrong. Notice the thoughts that show up when you feel tired, overwhelmed, or discouraged. Listen for phrases that sound familiar or automatic. Those thoughts are clues. They reveal what you believe to be true about yourself.

Sometimes awareness shows up as resistance. If you find yourself thinking, I don't have time to learn this, or this feels too hard, or I'll do this later when things calm down, that is not failure. That is information. Those thoughts are part of the story you've been living with. They point directly to the beliefs that need compassion and attention.

I used to struggle deeply with making time for myself. I believed self care came last. I would tell myself I would rest later, once everyone else was taken care of. Once the kids were okay. Once the house was in order. Once everything else was done. What I didn't realize at the time was that this belief was quietly teaching me that my needs mattered less.

That belief affected everything. My energy. My patience. My joy. My relationship with myself.

Self-love is not something you earn after you have done enough for others. It is something you practice so you can show up fully in your life. Taking time for yourself is not selfish. It is essential. It is how you refill your emotional reserves. It is how you reconnect with yourself. It is how you interrupt old patterns of neglect and overgiving. Self awareness helps you notice when you are abandoning yourself. Self love is choosing to return.

Showing Up Is Self Love in Action

Showing up for yourself does not have to be complicated. It can be simple and gentle. It can look like doing something that makes you feel good. Singing along to a song you love. Dancing in your kitchen. Reading a book that inspires you. Taking a walk. Doing yoga. Standing in the sunlight with your feet in the grass. Letting yourself feel calm, present, and alive.

These moments matter more than you realize. They teach your nervous system safety. They remind your mind that joy is allowed. They reinforce the belief that you are worthy of care, rest, and pleasure. Self awareness asks you to notice what you've been telling yourself. Self love invites you to choose something kinder. This work is about presence. It is about learning to listen to yourself with compassion and responding with care.

When you begin paying attention to your words and honoring your needs, you are not just changing thoughts. You are building a relationship with yourself. That relationship is the foundation for everything that follows.They reinforce the belief that you are worthy of care, rest, and pleasure. Because you do matter.

Self awareness asks you to notice what you've been telling yourself. Self love invites you to choose something kinder. And each time you do, you are rewriting your story

Words have always mattered to me. I've learned, grown, and healed through the words I've read, reflected on, and repeated to myself. Along the way, certain quotes stayed with me. They guided me when I felt uncertain, reminded me of what was possible, and helped shape how I think and move through life.

It didn't happen all at once. I'm still learning every day. But I came to understand something deeply important. It wasn't my circumstances that were holding me back as much as the stories I was telling myself.

I'm sharing these quotes with you because words create more than meaning. They create belief. They create momentum. And they can create real, lasting change.

Words to Carry With You: Self-Love, Self-Awareness, Becoming

"You are loved. You are enough. You are here for a reason."

— JEN SINCERO

"We are not held back by the love we didn't receive in the past, but by the love we're not extending in the present."

— MARIANNE WILLIAMSON

"Your job is to fall in love with the process of becoming the person you are meant to be."

— MARIE FORLEO

"When you recover or discover something that nourishes your soul and brings joy, care enough about yourself to make room for it in your life."

— JEAN SHINODA BOLEN

"Self-care is how you take your power back."

— LALAH DELIA

"You yourself, as much as anybody in the entire universe, deserve your love and affection."

— BUDDHA

"To love oneself is the beginning of a lifelong romance."

— OSCAR WILDE

"The relationship you have with yourself sets the tone for every other relationship you have."

— ROBERT HOLDEN

CHAPTER 2

BUILDING YOUR SELF-TALK HABITS FOR REAL LIFE

"You've been criticizing yourself for years and it hasn't worked. Try approving of yourself and see what happens."

— LOUISE HAY

Our thoughts become our habits, and our habits become our lives. Every action we take begins as a single thought. That's why creating mindful self-talk isn't just about feeling good. It's about reshaping the foundation of how we live. When you become aware of what you're saying to yourself, you begin to understand why you feel the way you do and why you act the way you do. Self-talk sits at the root of every behavior, decision, and emotion.

Your inner words shape how you respond to stress, how you treat your body, how you make decisions, what you think you deserve, and how willing you are to make changes. When self-talk goes unnoticed, it quietly runs the show. When you bring awareness to it, you create choice. That choice is where real change begins. Over time, intentional self-talk doesn't just improve your mood, it builds emotional stability, self-trust, and a sense of safety within yourself. These habits become the steady ground you return to, no matter what season you're in.

Understanding Your Inner Voice

Your inner voice didn't appear out of nowhere. It formed over time through experiences, relationships, beliefs, and patterns you absorbed long before you were aware of them. Some of it came from childhood, some from culture, some from past disappointments or moments where you learned to protect yourself. That voice often speaks automatically, repeating familiar phrases without asking for permission. It isn't the truth of who you are. It's simply a collection of learned responses.

And here's something important to know: it is not your job to monitor every thought or control every word that crosses your mind. That would be exhausting and unrealistic. Change doesn't happen by catching everything. It happens by noticing what shows up most often and gently choosing something more supportive when you can. Awareness is enough to begin shifting the pattern.

This practice is not about perfection or constant positivity. It's about building a relationship with your inner voice. One where you listen, pause, and respond with intention instead of judgment. Over time, those small moments of awareness add up. The voice softens. The language changes. And what once felt automatic becomes a choice you can return to again and again.

Becoming Who You Truly Are

Manifestation is often misunderstood. It is not about forcing outcomes, chasing things, or trying to control life. At its core, manifestation is about alignment. It is about becoming more fully yourself and allowing life to respond to that truth. You are not here to create a life that looks like someone else's. You are here to create a life that feels like you.

When you begin to listen to your inner voice, speak to yourself with kindness, and honor what genuinely matters to you, something shifts. You feel calmer. More grounded. More hopeful. Not because everything around you changes overnight, but because you are changing from the inside out.

That inner shift matters.

In this book, manifestation is not about attracting things. It is about creating the version of yourself you desire. The calmer version. The more confident version. The version who trusts herself. The version who accepts who she is while continuing to grow. As you feel better emotionally and become more self-aware and compassionate with yourself, your choices naturally begin to reflect that. Your energy changes. And your life responds.

There is only one you in the universe. There has never been another person with your voice, your experiences, your personality, or your way of seeing the world. Honoring that uniqueness is not selfish. It is essential. When you stop resisting who you are and begin allowing yourself to be fully expressed, life feels more aligned and less like a constant struggle.

Happiness plays an important role in this process. Not the kind that depends on everything going right, but the kind that comes from self-acceptance, presence, and trust. Feeling good is not something you earn later. It is a way of living that guides your decisions and shapes your experience now.

Many people describe this process as working with energy. Thoughts, emotions, and intentions all carry energy. When you move through life feeling calmer, more hopeful, and more connected to yourself, you participate in a natural flow of creation.

Some call this co-creating with the universe. Others call it source, spirit, or God. The language matters less than the understanding that you are not alone in this process.

This is an invitation to step into that awareness. To recognize your growth. To honor your feelings. To practice self-acceptance. And to trust that by becoming more aligned with yourself, you are already creating a life that feels more peaceful, meaningful, and true.You allow yourself to become who you are beneath fear, conditioning, and self-doubt.

This awareness doesn't live only in quiet moments or big reflections. It shows up in the middle of real life. In rushed mornings. In small choices. In the way you speak to yourself when no one else is listening. That's where self-talk becomes a practice.When things are busy, imperfect, or loud, your inner voice matters most.

So let's bring this work into everyday moments, starting with one of the most common and chaotic parts of the day: the morning.

Mornings in Chaos: Quick Affirmations for Busy Starts

If your mornings feel like chaos, misplaced socks, endless emails, too much to do, you're not alone. Alarms blare, pets paw, or kids call before you're even out of bed. Groggy and distracted, you race from room to room, sorting the day ahead. Finding a moment for yourself can seem impossible, but even hectic mornings have hidden pockets of space for intention.

Positive self-talk needs to be simple and easy to add to your daily ways of being. Practice them into routine tasks. While brushing your teeth, whisper, "Today I choose calm over chaos." Place a sticky note, "I am ready for what comes," on your mirror. Let it greet you without costing extra time. As you're making breakfast, repeat, "Energy flows through me," or "I am fueled by purpose." These small rituals set a positive tone, seamlessly blending with daily actions.

Micro-affirmations are quick sparks, seconds-long, softly spoken phrases or glances at reminders. Some days, that's all you get, yet it's enough. Over time, repeating one line shifts your inner talk from automatic stress to supportive encouragement.

Here are some short affirmations for the busiest mornings:

- I am grounded in this moment.
- Strength rises with each breath.
- My mind is clear and open.
- Peace begins with me. I embrace my uniqueness.
- I am ready for today. I am strong and capable.
- I am in control of my choices.

Specific moments may call for tailored phrases. After dropping off kids, try, "We will get there in our own way." For pre-Zoom jitters, "I bring value to every conversation." Find what feels like a gentle landing when you risk tipping over.

Pairing affirmations with micro-routines makes them automatic. Tie a phrase to actions. While tying shoes, "With each step, I move forward." Locking the door, "I am safe and prepared." Before checking your phone, read a digital affirmation first. This habit stacking lets new habits grow from what already exists, requiring little willpower.

Visual cues help when life is noisy. Create an affirmation card for your wallet or dashboard, or make a phone wallpaper with words that uplift. Each screen unlock becomes a reminder of your intention.

Pause and Check In

Before you start your day, ask yourself, *What am I telling myself this morning?* and *How am I feeling?* Are your first thoughts anxious or encouraging, calm or overwhelmed? Simply noticing is the first act of change.

Once you notice how you're feeling, remember this: you're not stuck there. You can flip the switch if you need to. Use positive self-talk. Listen to music that lifts your mood. Play a motivational book or podcast while you're getting ready. Saying a prayer can shift your focus. Take a few deep breaths and set an intention for how you want to feel. Do something, even something small, to create the energy you want to start your day with.

Even if you wake up tired, grumpy, or feeling like you have so much to do that you don't even want to get out of bed, you can still create a wonderful, happy day. Over time, you'll learn what works best for you. Be open to trying new ideas. Part of this is self-awareness, and part of it is self-discovery.

If you wake up feeling good, give yourself a big shout-out. Let yourself enjoy it. Feeling happy, grounded, and confident matters. Notice how good it feels to be in this space. Carry that energy with you. Let's go.

Stuck in Comparison: Reframing Your Inner Dialogue

Comparison is one of the fastest ways to disrupt your self-talk. It starts quietly, maybe while scrolling through photos or hearing about someone else's success, and suddenly your inner critic wakes up. You find yourself thinking, "She's doing better than me," or "Why can't I be more like that?" Those small thoughts quickly shift how you feel, deflated, distracted, or even ashamed, and that feeling shapes what you do next.

Comparison steals energy from growth. It moves your focus from your own path to someone else's highlight reel. This is where affirmations become powerful tools for grounding. When you catch yourself comparing, pause and notice your thoughts. You might not be able to stop the comparison immediately, but you can shift what comes next.

Try saying:

- "My path unfolds in its own time. I honor my timing."
- "There's enough room for all of us to shine."
- "I am proud of who I am and who I am becoming."

These aren't just comforting phrases. They're gentle boundaries for your mind. Every time you redirect comparison into compassion, you train your brain to support instead of sabotage.

Ask yourself:

- What story am I telling myself when I compare?
- Do I shrink or expand when I think that way?
- What truth could I choose instead?

Comparison can also reveal what matters to you. When envy stirs, it's often pointing to a deeper desire. Maybe you crave connection, creativity, or adventure. Instead of judging yourself, get curious. "What do I truly want that I see reflected in someone else?" This shifts comparison from criticism to clarity.

To reset after a comparison spiral, create a short ritual. Write down one thing you appreciate about yourself, or whisper a grounding affirmation like, "I am enough right now", or " I am unique". Then take one small action toward your own goals, send the email, make the plan, start the project. Turning awareness into action helps transform jealousy into motivation.

Over time, you'll notice fewer moments of self-judgment and more gratitude for your own timing. Your inner talk will move from "I'm behind" to "I'm on my way." That's the power of awareness. It rewrites your response before it rewrites your life.

Making Affirmations Stick: Habit Hacks for Everyday Practice

Habits run on a loop. Cue, routine, reward. Cue is a trigger. Routine is what you do. Reward is the feeling after. Use this for affirmations, and showing up becomes easier, even on hard days.

Choose cues from what you already do. Place an affirmation bookmark in your current read. Each open page reminds you, "You are resilient." Tech-savvy? Set a phone alarm labeled "You are powerful!" Let it interrupt your afternoon slump. Shape your environment. Post notes on the fridge or steering wheel so even ordinary moments become invitations to encouragement.

If guilt creeps in, remind yourself, "Every day I show up, I grow stronger." Habits wobble. That's human. The win lies in returning with compassion. Experiment with cues, sticky notes, alarms, or dinner-table affirmations. Play with it until it fits your life.

When You Forget: Gentle Reset Rituals for Returning to Your Practice

Lapses happen. Life interrupts or energy fades. You might plan daily affirmations only to forget or feel drained. Soon, days or weeks pass, and self-criticism sneaks in. "I've failed." But missing days doesn't erase your progress. Choose compassion over blame. When you notice the gap, say, "It's okay to start again."

Being gentle after a lapse may feel new. Old habits focus on mistakes, but reset rituals bring you back kindly. Try a five-breath reset. Close your eyes, inhale slowly, and with each breath softly repeat an affirmation, inviting calm, releasing tension. Light a candle if ritual soothes you and whisper, "I am here now."

If it helps, place a new affirmation note where you'll see it, your desk, laptop, or fridge. Each glimpse is an invitation to begin again. Affirmations fit anywhere. Waiting in line, driving, walking. Whisper patience or courage into these pauses. Tiny moments accumulate into invisible strength.

Remember, returning matters more than streaks. After a rough week, one reader reset with a shower and the words, "I am gentle with myself today." That single moment restored her hope.

If doubt returns, remind yourself, "Each time I restart, I strengthen my self-love." Growth isn't measured by unbroken progress, but by your willingness to come back to yourself again and again. The softer your return, the steadier your commitment becomes.

Your self-talk is your foundation. Every word you whisper, every phrase you replace with kindness, becomes part of your inner architecture. Habits take root slowly, but they grow strong with patience. The more you practice, the more your thoughts align with who you're becoming, a person who chooses intention over impulse, peace over perfection, and love over doubt.

Affirmations are gentle reminders that you can choose your direction every single day. What you think shapes how you feel. How you feel shapes what you do. And what you do, repeated over time, creates the life you live.

As you build this relationship with your inner voice, you'll begin to notice how even the smallest shifts in self-talk can create steadier ground beneath your feet.

Words to Carry With You

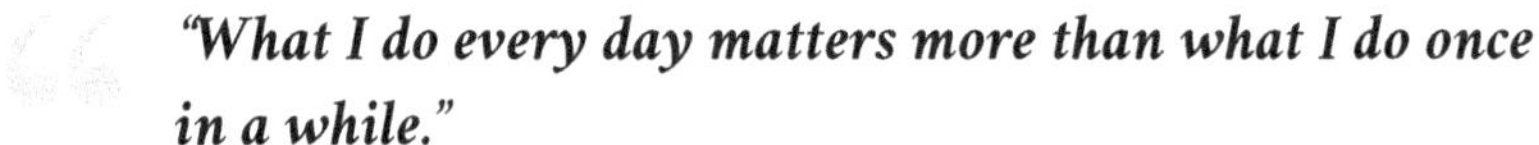

"What I do every day matters more than what I do once in a while."

— GRETCHEN RUBIN

"It's only a thought, and a thought can be changed."

— LOUISE HAY

"We will act consistently with our view of who we truly are, whether that view is accurate or not."

— TONY ROBBINS

"You do not rise to the level of your goals. You fall to the level of your systems."

— JAMES CLEAR

"Tiny changes aren't tiny. They're everything."

— BJ FOGG

"How we spend our days is, of course, how we spend our lives."

— ANNIE DILLARD

"Self-care is not a luxury. It is a discipline."

— AUDRE LORDE

"All you can change is yourself, and sometimes that changes everything."

— GARY W. GOLDSTEIN

CHAPTER 3

EMPOWERMENT
AND BELIEF

"Talk to yourself like you would to someone you love."

— BRENÉ BROWN

You can speak the kindest words in the world to yourself, but if your actions don't follow, the message never fully lands. Real self-love lives in what you do, not just what you say. It's in the quiet moments you choose rest over rushing, peace over pressure, and presence over perfection. Showing up for yourself is how words become truth.

Most of us move through our days meeting everyone else's needs first, family, work, friends, errands, often filling every available moment. Even when the things we are doing are good, meaningful, fun, educational, or in service to others, it is easy to overschedule ourselves without realizing it. We keep going until we collapse and then wonder why there is no energy left for ourselves.

When that happens, it is easy to feel lost or unfulfilled, even when life looks fine on the outside. What is often missing is not more purpose, but more presence. We stop listening to our inner signals that tell us when it is time to slow down, rest, or simply breathe. We do not have to learn everything or do everything all at once. There is time. And when we allow ourselves to move at a gentler pace, we actually enjoy our experiences more instead of rushing through them just to get to the next thing.

The truth is, when you stop showing up for yourself, you slowly drift away from your own joy. Choosing to slow down is not falling behind. It is how you reconnect with what truly matters.

This chapter is about bringing yourself back, through love in action.

When you give yourself time and care, you remind your body, mind, and spirit that you are important too. These moments don't have to be grand or time-consuming. In fact, the most powerful self-care often comes in small, consistent acts, taking a mindful walk, sitting quietly in the sun, stretching, or simply breathing deeply before you respond to a stressful moment.

Each time you do something kind for yourself, you send a powerful message. I am worth this time. I am worth this care.

The Energy of Intention

When you speak positive words like "I am worthy" or "I deserve peace," your next step is to live them. That means aligning your actions with your words. You can't declare self-worth while constantly running yourself into exhaustion. You can't say you deserve peace while ignoring your own needs.

True alignment happens when your choices match your words. If you tell yourself, "I am learning to love who I am," then you also need to create space to rest, to nourish, to reflect. That's how self-trust grows, by doing what you say you'll do, especially for yourself.

At first, showing up may feel awkward or indulgent. You might hear that inner voice whisper, "I don't have time for this," or "It's selfish." But self-care isn't selfish. It's a form of responsibility, the energy that sustains everything else you do.

Every word carries a vibration. Your intention is what gives it power.

When your words come from acceptance, "I'm doing my best today," they expand your energy. When they come from criticism, "I should be doing more," they constrict it.

Intentional language bridges who you are with who you're becoming.

Try using affirmations that embrace both:

- "I am doing my best for now; as I grow and learn, my best will become better."
- "I am learning to trust myself, even when I don't have all the answers."
- "I am both a work in progress and a masterpiece in motion."
- "I am worthy of care at every stage of becoming."
- "I choose peace, even while I grow."

Intentions don't need to be perfect. They need to be honest. Saying "I'm learning to accept where I am" is often more healing than pretending "Everything's fine." The goal is not to fake positivity but to guide your energy toward kindness and possibility.

When your thoughts, words, and actions align, you begin to trust yourself. You begin to feel safe in your own energy. You begin to live what you once only said.

The Cost of Neglect

When you ignore your own needs long enough, the disconnection shows up quietly at first, a heaviness in the morning, an ache in your shoulders, a tired sigh that becomes familiar. Then it deepens. You feel detached from joy, easily overwhelmed, unsure when you last felt truly rested or inspired.

Neglect is subtle. It doesn't always look like burnout; sometimes it looks like busyness. You fill your days with commitments and distractions, convincing yourself you're fine, but inside, something feels dim.

Your body knows before your mind admits it. Maybe you can't focus like you used to. Maybe everything feels like too much. You scroll more, sleep less, or keep saying "I'm okay" when you're not. These are signs that your energy reserves are running low.

Neglecting yourself doesn't mean you've failed. It means you've forgotten that you, too, deserve the same care you give others. Every part of you, your tired heart, your racing mind, your overextended body, is asking to be seen and soothed.

When you start listening, you'll hear what you've been missing. Rest, space, nature, laughter, gentleness. These are not luxuries. They are your lifelines back to balance.

The more you respond to those whispers, the stronger your connection becomes. Over time, your body and spirit learn to trust that you will listen before exhaustion sets in, that you will tend to your needs before breaking down. That trust is the foundation of emotional freedom and resilience.

Neglect takes time to unlearn, but each loving action is a new pattern forming, one that replaces survival with self-respect. You don't need to fix everything at once. You only need to start noticing where you've abandoned yourself and choose, gently, to come home again.

Small Daily Love Actions

Start small. You don't need to overhaul your entire routine to reconnect with yourself. Tiny, loving actions create lasting change because they teach your mind and body a new rhythm of care.

Take a few minutes each morning just for you. Sit quietly with your thoughts before checking your phone. Step outside and breathe in the crisp air before the day rushes in. Feel the sunlight touch your skin and remind yourself, "I am alive, I am present."

Move your body with kindness. Go for a walk not to burn calories but to feel your lungs expand. Go for a hike in nature, a bike ride, or roll out your mat for some pilates. Let movement feel like gratitude, not punishment. Tai Chi has become a new favorite.

Meditate, visualize, or simply breathe. A few mindful inhales can change your entire state of being. As you exhale, release the pressure to be perfect. As you inhale, receive calm and clarity. Each small act of care restores your spark. A glass of water, a nap, a good meal, a deep breath. These are how you return to yourself. They whisper, "I am still here."

Journaling can become a sacred pause, a way to connect with your inner voice before the world gets loud. Write what's real, not just what's right. Let your truth spill out, then respond to yourself with gentleness.

And yes, find joy. Little, daily, personal joy. Eat your favorite lunch, buy yourself fresh flowers, wear cozy socks, light a candle just because it feels good. Self-care doesn't have to be earned. It's a daily declaration. "I matter."

Try adding a few love-filled phrases throughout your day:

- "I give myself permission to rest."
- "I am learning to show up for me."
- "I am creating peace in small, steady ways."
- "I am enough, right now."
- "I choose to nourish my body and spirit."

These words become reminders that caring for yourself isn't optional. It's essential. Every act of love, no matter how simple, sends the message. I am on my own side.

Journaling as Self-Connection

Journaling isn't just writing; it's listening to your thoughts, your feelings, and your inner guidance. When you take the time to write things down, you create space between what you feel and how you respond.

You might start by simply asking yourself, *I am open to shifting these*:

- What am I feeling right now?
- What am I telling myself about this situation?
- What do I need to hear instead?

Use your journal to release frustration, self-doubt, or confusion, then gently replace those words with affirmations that lift you higher. For example, after venting "I feel overwhelmed and behind," follow it with, "I am doing my best and giving myself grace." This practice helps you see that your thoughts are not fixed truths; they're stories you have the power to rewrite.

You could also include a simple daily flow:

- **Release.** Write what's on your mind without editing or censoring yourself.
- **Reflect.** Circle one emotion or thought that stands out.
- **Reframe.** Write a supportive or affirming truth in response.

Over time, journaling becomes a conversation with your higher self, a check-in that gently reminds you to show up with love, patience, and compassion.

Recharging and Regrouping

Showing up for yourself also means giving yourself permission to rest. Rest isn't laziness. It's nourishment. It's how your nervous system resets, your mind clears, and your creativity returns.

We live in a world that glorifies busyness, where slowing down can feel unnatural or even guilt-inducing. But your worth isn't measured by your productivity. You don't need to earn your rest. Rest is how you refill your energy so you can keep growing with strength and clarity.

Make rest intentional. Create small rituals that signal your body to relax, soft music, a warm bath, gentle stretches, or a few slow breaths before bed. These acts remind your body it's safe to release, to soften, to receive care.

Sometimes recharging means stepping away for some quiet time, going for a jog or sitting quietly without reaching for your phone. Create a ritual that makes you feel good for regrouping. It might mean saying no to something that drains you or allowing yourself a slow morning. When you give yourself permission to pause, you reclaim your balance.

When you recharge regularly, you prevent burnout and rediscover balance. You become more grounded, more centered, and more at peace. The more you nurture yourself, the more resilient you become, not by doing more, but by allowing yourself to be.

Rest is not the absence of growth. It is what allows growth to continue. When you slow down, your body and mind integrate everything you've been learning. It's the quiet space where clarity is born and healing deepens.

Building a Relationship With Yourself

Think of this as a lifelong relationship, one built on love, kindness, acceptance, and trust. Every time you speak kindly to yourself or take a mindful action, you strengthen that bond. You start to feel more confident, more supported, and more whole.

It's easy to show love to others, but the relationship you build with yourself sets the tone for every other connection in your life. Begin each day by simply acknowledging yourself. Look in the mirror, smile, and say:

- "I love you."
- "I can do this."
- " I honor my feelings"
- "I am creating the life I want."

Give yourself a hug. Feel your own warmth and presence. Let it sink in that you are here, doing your best. If it feels silly at first, that's okay. Healing often does. Over time, those small gestures of love become powerful.

You might even blow yourself a kiss or wink at your reflection. These playful, loving moments rewire your brain to associate self-connection with joy rather than judgment. They say, "I am on my own team."

Every time you meet your own eyes with compassion, you tell your nervous system that you are safe, seen, and loved. That's how self-trust grows, not from perfection, but from consistent kindness.

When you truly show up for yourself, you begin to live in alignment. What you say, feel, and do all work together. That's when transformation happens. You begin to recognize that you are not waiting for love. You are already living it, through every word, thought, and action that honors who you are becoming.

Where Self-Love Becomes Practice

You don't need to wait for the perfect time or mood to start showing up for yourself. You can begin right now, in this moment, by taking one deep breath and saying, I am here for me.

Every small act of self-care is a quiet revolution. It tells the world, "I matter." It tells your mind, "I am worthy." And it tells your heart, "I am home."

This isn't about grand gestures or flawless routines. It's about daily acts of self-respect that keep your heart open and your spirit strong. When you choose yourself with love and intention, your inner world begins to.

Words to Carry With You

"One decision can change your day; a bunch of those can change your life."

— MEL ROBBINS

"The key to happiness is the decision to be happy."

— MARIANNE WILLIAMSON

"Happiness is neither virtue nor pleasure nor this thing or that, but simply growth. We are happy when we are growing."

— WILLIAM BUTLER YEATS

"You are the only person who thinks in your mind."

— LOUISE HAY

"Affirm the positive, visualize the positive, and expect the positive, and your life will change accordingly."

— REMEZ SASSON

"You are always one decision away from a totally different life."

— MARK BATTERSON

"Your life does not get better by chance, it gets better by change."

— JIM ROHN

"Believe you can, and you're halfway there."

— THEODORE ROOSEVELT

CHAPTER 4
WHEN YOU NOTICE, YOU CAN CHOOSE

"What you think, you become. What you feel, you attract. What you imagine, you create."

— RUMI

You've learned how to speak kindly to yourself and take loving action. Now it's time to focus on what those words and actions are creating, your energy. Every thought, emotion, and intention you carry radiates outward, influencing how you feel, how you respond, and what you attract.

The energy you hold becomes the atmosphere of your life. If you wake up already dreading the day, your thoughts mirror that heaviness. But if you wake with gratitude or even a quiet, *"I can handle what comes today,"* your energy shifts and your mind softens, your body relaxes, and you move differently through the world.

Positive focus isn't about pretending everything is perfect; it's about choosing where to place your awareness. What you give attention to expands. When you focus on what's wrong, your world feels smaller. When you focus on what's possible, it opens.

As Rumi said, *"What you think, you become."* In this chapter, you'll learn how to use that truth to re-center your energy through awareness, gratitude, and mindful attention. Use simple practices that help you stay grounded even on hard days.

You'll explore how to:

- Redirect negative thoughts before they spiral.
- Shift your emotional energy through breath and focus.
- Train your attention to see what's working rather than what's missing.
- Build a daily "energy reset" routine that supports calm, clarity, and joy.

Because once your focus changes, your life follows.

Awareness Before Change

Before you can shift your thoughts or energy, you have to notice where you are. Awareness is the doorway to transformation and it's how you catch the moment your thoughts begin to spiral, the instant your body tenses, or the tone in your voice changes. Without awareness, you can't redirect your energy; with it, you regain choice.

Start by simply checking in with yourself throughout the day.

Ask:

- What am I thinking right now? How do I feel?
- How does my body feel? Where do I feel it?
- What energy am I bringing into this space?
- How is my breathing?

There's no judgment in this. It's not about labeling thoughts as good or bad, but noticing what they create within you. Maybe you wake up feeling heavy, anxious, or distracted. Instead of rushing to fix it, pause and acknowledge it: *"I'm feeling tense today."* That single act of naming begins to loosen the hold of that energy.

Awareness is like turning on a light in a dark room. The furniture was always there, but now you can see it clearly enough to move around without bumping into it.

Once you know what you're feeling, you can decide what you want to feel instead.

Try gentle redirection phrases like:

- "I choose calm over chaos."
- "I'm open to a better feeling right now."
- "I am allowed to start over at this moment."

The power isn't in forcing positivity; it's in giving yourself permission to shift your focus. That's how your energy begins to realign.

Where Your Energy Goes

What you focus on grows. Your attention is like sunlight. Whatever you shine it on begins to bloom. If your thoughts constantly center on worry, lack, or self-criticism, that's what expands in your inner world. But when you choose to notice what's working, what's peaceful, or even what's possible, your mind shifts into alignment with growth, gratitude, and strength.

The mind doesn't know the difference between what's real and what's rehearsed, it believes what you continually feed it. If you keep telling yourself, *"I'm overwhelmed,"* your nervous system prepares for chaos. But if you pause and say, *"I can take one thing at a time,"* your body responds with calm focus.

You are constantly creating your emotional environment through what you pay attention to.

Think about a moment when you were running late and everything seemed to go wrong. The traffic lights, the slow driver, you can't find your phone. The more frustrated you felt, the more evidence appeared to justify that frustration. That's how energy works: what you focus on amplifies itself.

Now imagine that same situation approached differently. You take a breath, say, *"I can only do what I can do right now,"* and turn on a calming song. Your circumstances might not change instantly, but your internal state does and that shift changes how you experience the moment.

This is the essence of energetic awareness: learning to direct your focus toward what uplifts you instead of what drains you.

Try these simple focus-shifting practices throughout your day:

- **Gratitude Pause:** When you feel stress rising, stop and name one thing that's going right. The sun, flowers, people you love and who love you…there is always something.
- **Sensory Reset:** Close your eyes and take one slow breath. Notice a sound, a scent, or a texture around you that feels pleasant. This brings you back into the present moment.
- **Attention Anchor:** Choose a word or phrase like "ease," "peace," or "clarity." Whisper it when your mind begins to spiral.

Small shifts like these train your brain to notice the good, even in uncertainty. Over time, this becomes second nature.

When you change your focus, you change your frequency—and life starts reflecting that back to you.

When Awareness Feels Overwhelming

The first time I really started paying attention to my thoughts, it was… a lot. Suddenly, I was noticing every criticism, every fear, every sarcastic joke I made about myself. I realized how much of it came out on autopilot even in conversations with others. I'd laugh off mistakes or say something like, "Oh, typical me," or "I'm such a mess," without even thinking.

And when I finally *did* notice, I felt overwhelmed, almost embarrassed by how unkind I had been to myself without realizing it. It made me wonder: *How do I even begin to change all this?*

That awareness can hit hard at first. You start to see how much of your self-talk has been quietly shaping how you feel and what you believe about yourself. You may even feel guilty or discouraged, thinking, "Wow, I've been so negative," or "No wonder I feel stuck."

But please know that this awareness is not a failure. It's a breakthrough. It means you're finally waking up to what's been happening beneath the surface, and now you have the power to change it.

If you feel confused or unsure where to start, take a deep breath. You don't need to fix everything at once. This part of the journey is about *noticing*, becoming aware is progress. Those small moments of noticing create space for gentler thoughts, kinder words, and more compassionate responses.

That's part of why this book exists, to help this process feel a little less heavy and a lot more hopeful. So if you're in that phase right now, overwhelmed by your own awareness, let this chapter be your reminder: you're not doing it wrong. You're doing the brave work of waking up. Until now you have been doing your best, as you continue learning then your best will get better. Love all parts of you- past, present and future.

Shifting Emotional Energy Through Breath and Intention

Once you start noticing your thoughts and where your energy goes, the next step is learning how to gently shift it. Breath and intention are two of the simplest yet most powerful tools for that. You don't need fancy techniques or long meditations, just awareness and a willingness to pause.

Your breath is your body's built-in reset button. It's always with you, and it changes how your nervous system responds. When stress rises, your breathing often becomes shallow or quick, signaling danger to your body. But when you take slow, intentional breaths, you send the opposite message: *I am safe. I am grounded. I am okay. I can do this. I am learning.*

Try this simple pattern anytime you feel anxious or stuck:

1. **Inhale deeply for a count of four.**
   - Feel your belly rise and your chest expand.
2. **Hold the breath for a count of two.**
   - This pause allows your body to fully absorb oxygen.
3. **Exhale slowly for a count of six.**
   - Imagine releasing tension, letting go of what you no longer need.
4. **Repeat for three rounds.**
   - Notice how your body softens and your mind quiets.

Breathing this way is more than a relaxation tool, it's a declaration of self-trust. It says, "I can calm myself. I can choose peace."

Once your breath steadies, add intention. What do you want to feel more of right now? Calm, clarity, strength, forgiveness, hope? Let that word guide your inhale and exhale.

- As you breathe in, silently say: *I am breathing in peace.*
- As you breathe out: *I am releasing fear.*

Or:

- Inhale: *I welcome clarity.*
- Exhale: *I let go of confusion.*

These micro-moments of intentional breathing reconnect you with the present. They remind you that while you can't control everything around you, you can always guide your inner energy.

Visualization deepens this practice. Imagine breathing in warm, golden light energy that fills you with renewal. Picture the exhale carrying away grey mist, representing old worries or heavy thoughts. You can do this in the car, before a meeting, or while washing dishes. Each time you return to your breath, you're re-anchoring your energy to peace.

Even a few conscious breaths can transform your day. What once felt overwhelming starts to soften. You'll begin to notice that every time you pause to breathe with intention, you're training your body and mind to meet life with steadiness and grace.

Choosing Your Emotional Frequency

Every emotion carries energy. You can feel it in your body when you're anxious, heavy, calm, or joyful. These emotional states aren't random. They are responses to what you're thinking, what you're telling yourself, and where your attention is resting.

When you begin to notice your thoughts, use your breath, and set intention, you're already influencing your emotional frequency. This is where choice becomes powerful. You may not always be able to control what happens around you, but you can learn to influence how you respond. That response shapes how you experience your life.

Emotional frequency does not mean forcing yourself to be positive all the time. It is not about ignoring hard feelings or pretending everything is okay. It is about awareness and direction. You acknowledge where you are, then gently guide yourself toward where you want to be.

For example, stress might show up as tight shoulders, shallow breathing, or racing thoughts. Instead of judging that feeling or trying to escape it, you pause and say, "I notice I'm feeling overwhelmed right now." That awareness alone lowers the intensity. From there, you can choose a supportive response such as a deep breath, a reassuring phrase, or a moment of stillness.

The words you use in these moments matter deeply.

Compare the difference between these statements.

"I can't handle this."

vs.

"This feels hard, but I can take it one step at a time."

Both acknowledge difficulty, but only one supports calm and clarity. The second keeps you grounded and capable instead of reactive.

Your emotional frequency is shaped by the language you use internally. When your self talk is harsh or fearful, your energy contracts. When your words are compassionate and steady, your energy expands. These small choices create a baseline, a familiar emotional state you return to more easily.

You can begin to choose your emotional frequency by asking simple questions throughout the day.

Ask yourself:

- What am I feeling right now?
- What am I telling myself?
- Is this thought supporting peace or increasing tension?

If you notice frustration, you might gently shift to:

- "I'm allowed to pause."
- "I don't have to solve everything right now."
- "I can choose to be calm, at this moment."

If you feel sadness or heaviness, you might try:

- • "It's okay to feel this."
- • "I am being gentle with myself."
- • "I trust that this feeling will pass."

These are not affirmations meant to override emotion. They are a moment of steadiness, to stabilize you while emotions move through.

Gratitude is another powerful way to raise emotional frequency, even in small doses. You do not need to feel grateful for everything, just one thing. A warm drink. A quiet moment. A kind interaction. Gratitude redirects your attention without denying reality, and that redirection shifts your emotional energy almost immediately.

As you practice choosing your emotional frequency, you will notice something important. Your reactions soften. You recover faster. You feel more steady, even when life feels uncertain. It happens through repetition and kindness toward yourself.

Each moment you pause, breathe, and choose supportive words, you are tuning yourself to a calmer, clearer emotional state. And the more often you return there, the more natural it becomes.

This takes practice and every time you choose awareness over reaction, you are strengthening your ability to meet life with balance, resilience, and trust.

Words to Carry With You

"One small positive thought can change your whole day."

— ZIG ZIGLAR

"We are not held back by the love we didn't receive in the past, but by the love we're not extending in the present."

— MARIANNE WILLIAMSON

"All that I seek is already within me."

— LOUISE HAY

"Don't be pushed around by the fears in your mind. Be led by the dreams in your heart."

— ROY T. BENNETT

"We become what we think about."

— EARL NIGHTINGALE

"Awareness is the greatest agent for change."

— ECKHART TOLLE

"When you change the way you look at things, the things you look at change."

— WAYNE DYER

"Self-awareness gives you the capacity to learn from your mistakes as well as your successes."

— LAWRENCE BOSSIDY

CHAPTER 5

CHOOSING POSITIVITY, ONE THOUGHT AT A TIME

"Your life is determined not so much by what life brings to you as by the attitude you bring to life."

— MAYA ANGELOU

There comes a point in life when you realize that things do not always go as planned. Unexpected changes show up. Situations unfold that you never asked for and could not have prevented. Loss, disappointment, setbacks, and uncertainty are part of being human. When those moments happen, it can feel overwhelming, especially if you keep replaying the problem in your mind or retelling it over and over to others.

I know this feeling well. I noticed that when I repeated everything that went wrong, either in my thoughts or out loud, it didn't help me heal or move forward. Instead, it made everything feel heavier. The situation felt bigger. The sadness felt deeper. The spiral felt harder to stop. What I thought was venting often left me feeling worse than when I started.

Over time, I learned something important. Replaying the problem without intention doesn't release it. It reinforces it.

That realization didn't come from pretending everything was fine. It came from paying attention to how my words were affecting my emotional state. I began to notice that the way I talked to myself during hard moments mattered just as much as the situation itself. My inner dialogue either kept me stuck or helped me steady myself.

Choosing positivity is not about denying pain or forcing a smile. It is about deciding how much energy you will give to what is hurting you. It is about choosing to support yourself instead of tearing yourself down while you walk through something difficult.

One of the biggest shifts I made was changing the questions I asked myself.

Instead of asking, "Why does this always happen to me," I began asking, "What can I learn from this."

Instead of thinking, "I can't handle this," I practiced saying, "This is hard, and I can find my way through it."

Instead of spiraling into fear, I reminded myself, "I recognize this is tough, and I trust myself to get through it."

Those questions didn't erase the problem, but they changed my relationship with it. They slowed my thoughts. They softened my body. They gave me a sense of steadiness instead of panic. That shift alone made everything feel more manageable.

Learning to pause in the middle of difficulty is a skill. It doesn't happen all at once. It happens one moment at a time, when you choose awareness instead of reaction. That is where positivity begins, not as a feeling, but as a practice.

Choosing Positivity in the Moment

The next time something difficult happens, pause and gently walk yourself through this simple process.

- Ask yourself
    - What am I thinking right now?

Notice how that thought makes you feel in your body. Listen to what words you are using.

Then choose a softer, steadier response.

- You might say
    - "This is uncomfortable, but I am safe."
    - "I don't have to solve everything right now."
    - "I can take this one step at a time."

Life will always bring challenges. That part is unavoidable. But how you respond internally makes all the difference. When you choose calmer, more productive thoughts, you give yourself space to breathe. You give yourself the emotional support you need to keep going.

As you begin choosing positivity more often, something important starts to happen. You begin to notice more of what is working. You begin to see opportunities instead of only obstacles. You start finding evidence that supports calm instead of fear.

We tend to find what we are looking for. When we search for everything that is wrong, we will find it. When we begin looking for growth, learning, or meaning, those begin to appear as well. Choosing positivity is not about ignoring reality. It is about deciding which parts of reality you will give your energy to.

Positivity taught me that my words are energy. When I choose words that calm and reassure me, my energy shifts. When I choose words that keep me grounded, I feel stronger. When I choose words that focus on solutions instead of spirals, I feel more capable.

One of the most helpful tools I found was having something steady to return to when my thoughts started racing. That is where a personal mantra can be incredibly grounding.

Creating Your Personal Positivity Mantra

A powerful way to support yourself during hard moments is to create a personal mantra. This is not about pretending everything is okay. It is about reminding yourself who you are becoming.

Take a few minutes and write a sentence that feels true and steady for you right now.

Some examples:

- "I am learning how to handle challenges with calm and clarity."
- "I am doing my best, and that is enough for today."
- "I trust myself to move forward, even when I feel unsure."
- "I am becoming more grounded with each experience."

Choose one phrase and keep it close. Repeat it when your thoughts start to spiral. Let it become your anchor when emotions rise and return to the same supportive words again and again until they feel familiar and safe.

Choosing positivity is a conscious decision. It doesn't mean the situation is easy. It means you are deciding not to give it unlimited power over your emotional well-being. You are choosing to conserve your energy for healing, problem-solving, and growth.

You are allowed to say, "This is hard," and still believe, "I will get through it."

You are allowed to acknowledge disappointment while holding onto hope.

You are allowed to feel sadness without living there.

Positivity is about where you place your attention. You can focus on what went wrong, or you can gently redirect your focus toward what you want to create next. You can choose to speak in ways that build you back up instead of break you down. You can decide to support the person you are becoming, even when the path feels uncertain.

Lasting personal change doesn't come from one positive thought or one good day. It comes from repetition. From gently choosing supportive thoughts again and again, even when it feels uncomfortable or unfamiliar. The more often you pause, notice, and redirect your thinking, the more natural it becomes. With practice, positivity shifts from something you try to do, into something you automatically return to. This is how new habits are formed through consistency and compassion.

Choosing positivity is choosing yourself. It is choosing to believe that even in difficult moments, there is still growth, learning, and meaning unfolding. It is choosing to meet hardship with steadiness instead of self-criticism. And sometimes, that choice is the very thing that carries you through when hope feels fragile.

Words to Carry With You

"Your words are powerful. They shape your thoughts, your beliefs, and ultimately your reality."

— LISA NICHOLS

"You may not control all the events that happen to you, but you can decide not to be reduced by them."

— MAYA ANGELOU

"With the new day comes new strength and new thoughts."

— ELEANOR ROOSEVELT

"Whatever you give out in life is what you receive back."

— IRENE C. KASSORLA

"Thoughts become things. If you see it in your mind, you will hold it in your hand."

— BOB PROCTOR

"Whatever you hold in your mind on a consistent basis is exactly what you will experience in your life."

— TONY ROBBINS

"We become what we think about. Energy flows where attention goes."

— RHONDA BYRNE

"Positive thinking will let you do everything better than negative thinking."

— ZIG ZIGLAR

CHAPTER 6
WORDS CREATE MOTIVATION
THOUGHTS INTO ACTION

"Your thoughts and your words are the paintbrushes that create the canvas of your life"

— LISA NICHOLS

There comes a moment when something shifts inside you, when you realize you're no longer just thinking about change, you're ready to move. It's not loud or dramatic. It's quiet, almost subtle. You begin to realize that the words you've been choosing are no longer just comforting ideas you repeat to feel better. They are becoming invitations. Invitations to move, to try, to trust yourself, and to step forward into the life you've been quietly imagining.

Up to this point, you've been learning how to notice your thoughts, soften your self talk, show up for yourself, and choose your emotional energy with intention. That inner work matters deeply. It creates awareness. It builds self trust. It reconnects you to your intuition and to the truth of who you are becoming. Without this foundation, action feels forced or overwhelming. With it, action begins to feel possible.

Now comes the natural next step. Action.

Action is not separate from self love. It is self love in motion. When you take action that aligns with the words you are speaking to yourself, something powerful happens. Your confidence grows because you are proving to yourself that you can follow through. Your identity begins to shift because you are no longer just thinking differently, you are living differently. You stop waiting to feel ready and start realizing that readiness is built by doing.

Every action you take begins as a thought. That thought becomes a word. That word becomes a decision. And that decision becomes action. This is how change becomes real and lasting. You do not need to overhaul your entire life to begin. You only need to take one step that matches the truth you are learning to believe about yourself.

When you say, "I am capable," action might look like trying something new, even if your voice shakes.

When you say, "I trust myself," action might look like making a decision without over-explaining it.

When you say, "I am creating a life that feels good to me," action might look like setting a boundary, starting a habit, or allowing yourself to be seen. Action requires willingness.

And before choosing your next step, it helps to clearly understand where you are standing. Writing your thoughts down allows you to release them and see them with more clarity. If you're unsure how to answer the questions, just begin. Even guessing often opens the door to what you're truly feeling. The clarity comes through the process, not before it.

Checking In With Yourself: Journaling

Before you decide where you want to go, it's important to clearly see where you are right now. This is not about judging yourself or picking apart your life. It's about awareness, honesty, and compassion. When you understand your current reality, you can set intentions that truly support your growth.

Set aside a quiet moment. Take a few slow breaths. Let yourself answer honestly, without trying to sound positive or put together. This is just for you.

Begin by writing freely to these questions:

- Where in my life do I feel most fulfilled right now?
  - What feels supportive, steady, or aligned?
- Where do I feel stuck, restless, or disconnected?
  - What feels heavy or draining my energy?
- What patterns do I notice repeating in my thoughts or behaviors?
  - Which ones feel supportive and which ones feel ready to change?
- How do I currently speak to myself when things feel hard?
  - What tone does my inner voice take?
- What parts of my life feel ready for movement or change?
  - Where do I sense a quiet desire to grow or expand?
- What have I been avoiding because it feels uncomfortable or uncertain?
  - What might shift if I allowed myself to take one small step?

As you write, remember this. Awareness is progress. Simply seeing the truth of where you are is an act of self respect. When you finish, read what you wrote with kindness.

Setting Intentions From Truth

Now that you've taken inventory, you can begin to choose your direction with clarity. Intentions are not rigid goals. They are guiding energies. They help your mind, heart, and actions move in the same direction.

Ask yourself:

- How do I want to feel as I move forward?
  - What kind of energy do I want to bring into my days?
- What qualities do I want to grow more of in my life?
  - Calm, confidence, courage, clarity, joy, trust?
- What kind of person am I becoming through the choices I make now?

Write one or two simple intention statements such as:

- I am creating a life that feels grounded and aligned.
- I am choosing actions that support who I am becoming.
- I am open to growth and willing to take the next step.

These intentions become a grounding point. You return to them when fear shows up or motivation wavers.

Many women wait for confidence before they move forward. What most of us learn through experience is that confidence grows because we move forward. Each small action sends a message to your nervous system that you are safe to try, safe to grow, safe to expand. That message builds trust within you.

Motivation is not something you either have or do not have. Motivation is created when your actions align with your values.

When what you do matches what you say matters to you, energy follows. Movement creates momentum. Momentum creates belief.

Think about a time when you followed through on something small. Maybe you went for a walk even though you did not feel like it. Maybe you spoke up when you normally would have stayed quiet. Maybe you started something you had been thinking about for a long time. That feeling afterward was not accidental. It was your body and mind responding to alignment.

Affirmations for Confidence and Forward Movement

As you begin to take action and shift old patterns, your words matter more than ever. These affirmations are meant to support you as you move, try, and grow.

Read them slowly. Write down the ones that resonate. Repeat them when you feel unsure.

- I trust myself to take the next right step.
- I am allowed to grow at my own pace.
- Each action I take builds confidence and clarity.
- I am learning through experience and becoming stronger.
- I do not need to have everything figured out to begin.
- I believe in myself enough to try.
- I am creating momentum through small, intentional actions.
- I am proud of myself for showing up and moving forward.

Let The Words Sink In

Let these words walk with you. Let them soften fear and strengthen resolve. Any action makes a difference. It requires presence and willingness. Every step you take in alignment with your truth reinforces the life you are creating.

This is how words become motivation. This is how motivation changes. Return to these words when hesitation shows up or when you're standing at the edge of a decision."

Each aligned action reinforces the story you are writing about yourself. Once you find affirmations that feel steady and true for you, let yourself get creative with them. These powerful "I've got this" phrases work best when they become part of your everyday environment. Write them on sticky notes and place them where you'll naturally see them throughout the day, on your bathroom mirror, in your car, on your fridge, on your desk, at your workspace.

Seeing supportive words regularly helps reinforce new thought patterns. You can also memorize your favorites so they're available the moment doubt or hesitation shows up. Some days, repeating one strong phrase quietly to yourself is enough to shift your energy and restore confidence.

There are also wonderful tools available to support this practice. Apps like Breethe and Perfectly Happy offer affirmations, meditations, visualizations, and reminders you can customize to fit your needs. Setting gentle prompts throughout the day allows you to intentionally flood your mind with encouragement and reassurance. These small moments of repetition help rewire old patterns and strengthen new ones. These words will begin to feel familiar, supportive, and grounding, reminding you again and again that you are capable, supported, and moving forward with intention.

Becoming more fully yourself happens in moments. Moments when you choose to take the next step instead of staying still. Moments when you let your words guide your behavior. Moments when you decide that growth is something you participate in, not something you wait for.

What you are learning here is not about becoming someone new. It is about becoming more fully yourself.

Many women arrive at this point in their lives feeling in between. You may be releasing an old version of yourself, questioning what feels true now, or learning how to trust your inner voice again after loss, burnout, or a major transition. That space can feel uncertain. It can feel uncomfortable. But it is also where clarity begins to form.

To move forward you need willingness. Willingness to listen to yourself. Willingness to take one small step. Willingness to act in alignment with the words you are choosing, even when the outcome is not fully clear. That willingness creates momentum. And momentum restores hope.

The Words Create Movement Cycle

Think → Speak → Feel → Choose → Act → Become

Think
What you focus on and believe about yourself
→ Speak
The words you repeat internally and out loud
→ Feel
The emotional energy those words create
→ Choose
The decisions you make from that emotional state

→ **Act**
The steps you take, big or small
→ **Become**
The person you grow into through repeated action

With every intentional choice, you reinforce a powerful truth. You can trust yourself. Your words are not just thoughts passing through your mind. They are signals that guide your actions and shape your direction.

This is about recognizing that motivation grows through alignment. When your words support your values and your actions honor your intentions, movement feels natural. Confidence builds. Clarity follows.

You are not here to force transformation.
You are here to step into it with purpose.

When your words create movement, life responds. And each aligned action strengthens the belief that you are capable, supported, and already becoming who you are meant to be.

Words to Carry With You

"Our thoughts become our words, our words become our beliefs, our beliefs become our actions."

— JEN SINCERO

"It's pretty simple. The action you take will determine the results you achieve."

— TONY ROBBINS

"The only thing standing between you and everything you've ever wanted is one word: action."

— LISA NICHOLS

"You have the power to heal your life, and you need to know that."

— LOUISE HAY

"Become the person who would naturally do the things you want to do."

— BOB PROCTOR

"Do the thing you think you cannot do."

— ELEANOR ROOSEVELT

"You are always one decision away from a completely different life."

— MEL ROBBINS

"What you do today can improve all your tomorrows."

— RALPH MARSTON

CHAPTER 7

DETERMINATION

WHEN BELIEF
TURNS INTO ACTION

"I choose to make the rest of my life the best of my life."

— LOUISE HAY

Determination is not about pushing harder. It's about choosing words that keep you moving forward when it would be easier to stop. Limiting beliefs are self-imposed barriers absorbed from family, society, or past setbacks that quietly shape decisions without our notice. Persistent doubts might sound like, "I'm not the type to start over," or "People like me don't get those chances." These thoughts slip in unnoticed but strongly influence us, keeping us playing small. Repeated often, they become self-fulfilling prophecies unless we become aware.

For women, these beliefs may be, "I'm too old to go back to school," "Success isn't for me," or "I'm not creative enough." These aren't fleeting worries. They're ingrained scripts, steering actions and limiting potential. Importantly, these old stories are not facts. They are learned habits of thought. With practice, they can change.

To spot hidden limits, pick an area where you feel stuck, such as a new career, a business idea, or the urge to speak up more confidently. Ask yourself, "What dream have I dismissed as 'not for me,' and why?" Notice which belief rises to the surface. This process isn't about blame. It's about curiosity. Naming the actual barrier often softens its power.

Most people ignore these doubts or drown them out with activity, but writing them down brings clarity. Ask yourself where these beliefs started. A teacher's comment. Family expectations. Watching others succeed while you waited. Understanding the source helps you challenge the belief instead of accepting it as truth.

Next, shift your thinking through targeted affirmations. You don't have to move from doubt to certainty. Start with realistic, growth-oriented statements such as:

- I am open to growing beyond old limits.
- I can learn new skills at any stage in life.
- I welcome challenges that stretch my comfort zone.

Repeat these words with purpose. When an old belief surfaces, counter it with your new affirmation. For example, replace "People like me don't get that opportunity" with "I am worthy of opportunities that excite me." Consistency transforms the inner narrative.

You can also work with affirmations like these:

- My past doesn't define my future.
- Each day I make choices that move me closer to my dreams.
- I trust myself to keep going, even when progress feels slow.
- I am building confidence through small, intentional steps.
- I stay committed to my growth, even when it feels uncomfortable.

Interactive Exercise: Breakthrough Beliefs Journal

Use this exercise to bring awareness to what's been holding you back and begin rewriting the story.

- Write one dream or goal you've quietly dismissed as "not for me."
- Identify the limiting belief beneath it, such as "I'm too old" or "People like me don't get promoted."
- Create a personal affirmation that challenges this belief.
- For one week, repeat your affirmation daily, especially when doubt shows up.
- After a week, reflect. Did anything shift? All progress counts.

Naming your blocks and choosing new words can redirect your path. Old beliefs don't get the final say. Each time you choose a supportive affirmation, you create space for new possibilities and strengthen your determination to keep going.

Determination Grows Through Understanding

When I was learning all of this, I noticed something important. Some days felt easier than others. On days when I was rested, focused, and had space to think, it felt easier to use supportive words and stay grounded. But when my schedule was full, when I was tired, overwhelmed, or emotionally stretched, it was much easier to fall back into old habits and negative patterns.

I remember wondering why it seemed so hard for me. Why can't I just be normal like other people? Why can't I follow through, make changes, and feel better already? I knew what I wanted. I wanted peace. I wanted confidence. I wanted to feel lighter inside. But I didn't yet know how to get there.

This way of thinking was new to me. I was learning an entirely different relationship with my thoughts and emotions. And at times, I felt frustrated with myself. I even thought, I can't do this right either. That voice wasn't truth. It was simply another old pattern showing up.

What changed everything was getting clear on my why.

I stopped focusing only on what I wanted to fix and started focusing on who I wanted to become. I asked myself how I truly wanted to feel. How I wanted to show up in my life. What kind of example I wanted to set. At first, that clarity was deeply connected to my four kids. I wanted to be calmer. More present. More emotionally steady for them.

Over time, something shifted. That desire slowly became about me too. I wanted a life that felt more peaceful and fulfilling. I wanted to believe that happiness was possible for me, not just for other people.

Once I had that clarity, my determination grew.

I didn't change overnight. But I became committed. I started surrounding myself with reminders. Sticky notes went everywhere. I read books. I listened to podcasts. I paid attention to the words I was repeating. I was building belief, piece by piece, that change was possible and that life did not have to feel so hard.

What I eventually realized was this. It wasn't life that was working against me. It was my perspective. My limiting beliefs. My unconscious patterns. Once I saw that, I stopped blaming myself and started supporting myself.

Determination didn't come from forcing change. It came from understanding myself. It came from compassion. It came from believing that even small steps mattered. And with that belief, my commitment grew stronger and stronger.

This is what determination really looks like. Not constant motivation. But clarity, patience, and the willingness to keep showing up for yourself even when it feels messy.

Staying the Course for Long-Term Goals

Long-term goals can feel endless, requiring more patience than you thought possible. You start out energized, but as weeks turn to months, that initial excitement fades. The end blurs. Writing that book begins to feel impossible. Training for a marathon feels daunting. Building savings can seem insurmountable. Motivation does not always arrive when needed. Instead, you face the daily grind, showing up repeatedly even when progress feels invisible.

What makes these slow-burn dreams tricky are the silent setbacks. Hitting a plateau or dealing with life's distractions can make the temptation to quit feel loud. You may question, "Is this worth it?" or "Am I getting anywhere?" In these moments, supportive words ground you. They are reminding you why you started and keeping your purpose alive. My favorite mantra is, "Every small action brings me closer to my vision." Even when progress seems slow, this nudge helps you keep going.

Staying motivated means being clear on why your goal matters, not just at the outset, but throughout the process. When your energy drops, pause and recall what originally lit your spark. Was it seeing your name on a cover? Finishing a race? Building stability for your family? Write these reasons somewhere visible and pair them with an affirmation like, "I trust the timing of my process." These words act as a compass when distractions abound.

Another key is future self affirmations. Speaking from the viewpoint of the woman who has already reached her goal encourages your brain to believe. Instead of saying, "I hope I'll finish," try, "My future self thanks me for showing up today," or, "I become the woman I want to be with every step." This shifts your mindset from wishful thinking to embodied belief.

To sustain goals, rituals matter more than bursts of inspiration. Try a weekly check-in. Set aside ten minutes to ask yourself: What moved forward? Where did I struggle? What can I celebrate? Use an affirmation that reflects your commitment :

- "I am patient with slow progress. I am building something lasting."
- "I am building something valuable, one step at a time."
- "Keep going. Each choice matters."
- "I trust the process I am committed to."

You can also set calendar alerts to encourage you midweek with messages like, "Keep going. Each choice matters." Visual cues help determination become part of your day.

When setbacks pile up, pause before quitting. Progress is not always linear. Remind yourself, "My pace is perfect for me." If frustration grows, breathe and return to your why. Intentional words such as, "I am resilient through every challenge," or, "My vision is worth the wait," can turn discouragement into determination.

Over time, these simple habits affirming purpose, checking in weekly, and using future-focused language build resilience. The path will twist, but each repetition strengthens belief in your ability to finish. Long-term goals demand faith, patience, and steady self-encouragement, qualities that grow each time you refuse to give up.

Imposter Syndrome, Meet Your Match

Imposter syndrome often appears just as you step into something new or meaningful. That quiet inner whisper questions your achievements and suggests you're somehow deceiving others just by being present. This feeling is common for women stepping into new jobs, leading meetings, or launching projects that matter to them. The inner voice asks, Do I really know what I'm doing? or Will they find out I don't belong? Doubt lingers, insisting success is luck rather than skill.

This experience is especially common for women in spaces with high expectations or limited representation. Imposter syndrome often traces back to early messages, stereotypes, or moments of feeling unseen. It can cause hesitation to speak up, second-guessing ideas, or discomfort receiving praise. New mothers experience it too, surrounded by advice and comparison, wondering if everyone else knows something they don't. You may replay decisions in your mind, bracing for judgment that never actually comes.

Your self-talk is powerful because it cuts through the noise with truth. When the inner voice says you're a fraud, answer it with intention: I earned my place at the table. Repeat it before meetings or interviews. If comparison creeps in, remind yourself: My voice and ideas are valuable. If you feel the need to constantly prove yourself, return to: I am qualified to be here, just as I am. These phrases act as anchors, gently redirecting your focus back to your real skills and effort.

Hearing other women's stories can bring relief. A tech leader once recalled her first board meeting among seasoned male executives. She felt panic, convinced she would be exposed as inexperienced, but grounded herself with the thought, I've worked for this. I belong here. Though the nerves remained, that anchor allowed her to speak. Later, she learned that nearly everyone in the room had once felt the same way. Another woman, a new mother, shared how she doubted her instincts amid constant advice. I am the right mother for my child, becoming her steady reminder, helping her trust herself over time.

Imposter syndrome is a thinking pattern, and patterns can be interrupted. One helpful practice is learning to separate facts from feelings. When self-doubt rises, write down three things you're proud of, big or small. Finishing a task, staying committed, or navigating a hard moment with care all count. Then remind yourself: My feelings are valid, but they don't define my abilities. Grounding yourself in evidence helps restore clarity.

Keep a simple record of positive feedback, kind words, or moments you felt proud. When imposter syndrome surfaces, return to these reminders as proof that you belong. Create a folder, a note, or a journal page that reflects your growth.

Even women at the top have faced these doubts. What sets them apart isn't the absence of fear, but the willingness to keep showing up anyway. Your worth is not up for debate. The table isn't complete without your voice, your perspective, and your story.

Celebrating Small Wins

A transformation occurs when you start to honor progress in real time. Motivation grows by noticing small wins. Often, we wait for big milestones to feel pride, but truthfully, those milestones are built from stacked daily victories. Resilience grows from celebrating every step, not just major finishes. What gets celebrated, gets repeated. Shining light on your efforts, teaches your mind to see success everywhere. This maintains your determination.

Affirmations help support this mindset. Words like, "I honor myself for every effort today, big or small," remind you that your actions matter, regardless of visibility. Another: "Progress is progress no matter the pace." These set the standard at effort and showing up. Each use strengthens your belief that effort itself is valuable. When you believe this, continuing through setbacks gets easier.

Celebrating daily progress doesn't require elaborate rituals. A small acknowledgment can be enough. A quick self-high-five, a moment of gratitude, or quietly saying, "I'm proud I followed through," reinforces that your effort matters. The point isn't public praise. It's recognizing yourself for showing up.

Tracking wins is a simple way to build this habit. Keep a small "wins" journal nearby and, at the end of the day, write down a few things you followed through on. They don't have to be big. Maybe you took a short walk, paused before reacting, chose kinder words, or completed something you'd been avoiding. These moments count.

Over time, this practice builds authentic confidence. It gives your mind real evidence that you are moving forward, even when things don't move as quickly as you hoped. When you notice and honor your effort, you strengthen self-trust and resilience. Small wins, repeated consistently, quietly shape a steadier, more grounded sense of progress.

If there's one thing I hope you take with you, it's this: you are allowed to change. You are allowed to grow at your own pace. And you are allowed to believe that your life can feel lighter, calmer, and more aligned than it once did.

Learning to work with your words is about noticing, choosing again, and continuing forward with compassion when old patterns return. That is how real change happens. Take what resonates. Leave what doesn't. And trust yourself enough to keep going. You are here to become more fully yourself. And you are doing it right now.

Words to Carry with You

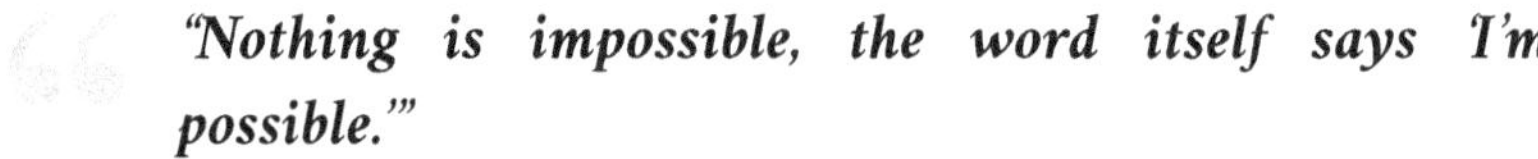

"Nothing is impossible, the word itself says 'I'm possible.'"

— AUDREY HEPBURN

"You have power over your mind, not outside events. Realize this, and you will find strength."

— MARCUS AURELIUS

"The only thing standing between you and your goal is the story you keep telling yourself as to why you can't achieve it."

— JORDAN BELFORT

"Little by little, one travels far."

— J.R.R. TOLKIEN

"It always seems impossible until it's done."

— NELSON MANDELA

"Action is the foundational key to all success."

— PABLO PICASSO

"You don't have to be great to start, but you have to start to be great."

— ZIG ZIGLAR

"Decide what you want. Believe you can have it. Believe you deserve it. Then take action."

— JACK CANFIELD

CHAPTER 8

SELF-LOVE

YOUR FOUNDATION

> *"Your only obligation in this lifetime is to be true to yourself."*
>
> — RICHARD BACH

Self-love gets talked about a lot, but what does it actually mean to *you*? Do you feel it in the way you speak to yourself, or does the idea feel uncomfortable, even foreign? Maybe you were taught that loving yourself was selfish, or something you had to earn by doing more, being better, or putting everyone else first. Or maybe you've never really stopped to ask whether you even like yourself at all. This is an invitation to slow down and explore that honestly, without judgment, pressure, or pretending.

Happiness is not a constant rush or high. It is calm. It is contentment. It is a sense of ease within yourself. It is waking up with trust instead of tension and moving through your day with a steady knowing that you are supported from within. That kind of happiness grows naturally when you learn to speak to yourself with respect and care.

This is where self-love comes in.

Self-love is a relationship. It is how you treat yourself in quiet moments. It is the tone of your inner voice. It is how you respond to yourself as you grow, learn, and expand. Self-love is grounded. It is steady. It is supportive. It creates an inner environment where growth feels natural and sustainable.

When you practice self-love, your energy shifts. Your body settles. Your thoughts become clearer. Your decisions come from trust rather than pressure. You move through life with deeper confidence because you know who you are.

When you feel solid within, you make choices that reflect care, alignment, and clarity. You trust your own guidance and move forward from a grounded place. Becoming the version of you who feels at ease receiving is not something you have to force. She already exists, and she grows stronger each time you choose words that support her.

This chapter is about strengthening that connection. It is about choosing words that reinforce self-trust. It is about speaking to yourself in a way that reflects your worth. It is about recognizing which thoughts lead from love and expansion, and allowing those thoughts to guide your choices. Every time you choose words that support, encourage, and honor you, you strengthen the foundation from which everything else grows.

What Does That Even Look Like?

There was a time when I didn't really know who I was. I had titles. I had roles. I had responsibilities. But underneath all of that, I wasn't fully sure who *I* was. Not because anything was wrong, but because I had never stopped long enough to pause and ask that question in an honest way. It was actually uncomfortable at first.

Self-love naturally leads to self-discovery. Once you begin speaking to yourself with respect and intention, curiosity follows. You start noticing what feels true to you and what no longer fits. You begin to recognize that knowing yourself is not about labels or achievements. It is about awareness. Self-discovery is the process of reconnecting with the whole of who you are.

The playful parts. The thoughtful parts. The serious, silly, curious, creative, quiet, expressive, and evolving parts. None of these need to compete with each other. They are not contradictions. They are layers.

There is no one else in the world who sees life the way you do, processes experiences the way you do, or brings your perspective into every space you enter. Your interests, passions, sense of humor, ways of learning, thinking, feeling deeply, and expressing yourself are uniquely yours. This is not something to edit or minimize. It is something to recognize and allow.

Self-discovery begins when you stop trying to narrow yourself and start letting yourself expand.

You may realize you enjoy being both reflective and playful. Focused and spontaneous. Grounded and imaginative. You may discover interests you set aside or parts of yourself you never gave room to develop. That is not regression. That is integration.This stage is not about reinventing yourself. It is about uncovering what has always been there.

As you explore who you are, questions begin to shift. Instead of asking, *Who should I be?* you start asking, *What feels true to me?* Instead of looking outward for direction, you begin listening inward. Your values become clearer. Your preferences become easier to honor. Your choices begin to feel more aligned.

Self-discovery is not a one-time realization. It is an ongoing relationship. The more permission you give yourself to be fully you, the more grounded and confident you become. And that confidence does not come from proving anything. It comes from knowing yourself.

From here, loving yourself stops being abstract. It becomes practical. You choose differently because you understand yourself better. You speak differently because your inner language reflects who you are. You live differently because your life begins to match your truth.

This is where self-love becomes real.

Self-Acceptance: Honoring Your Whole Experience

Self-love includes self-acceptance, and self-acceptance means honoring everything you have lived, felt, and experienced up to this point in your life. Not judging it. Not rewriting it. Not arguing with it. Simply acknowledging it.

Your feelings are not good or bad. They just are, until you label them with words. The meaning you give a feeling shapes how you experience it. When you meet your emotions with compassion instead of criticism, you stay grounded in the present rather than pulled into the past.

Self-love looks like recognizing, *That was hard*, without turning it into self-blame. It looks like acknowledging difficult memories and saying, *I survived that. I learned something. I am still here.* There is no benefit in shaming yourself with questions like, *Why did I do that? Why did that happen?* Those questions keep you stuck in judgment rather than growth.

At every point in your life, you did the best you could with what you knew, what you had, and what you understood at the time. That truth matters. And it creates freedom. Now you know more. You see more. You have more awareness. And with that awareness comes choice.

When feelings rise, you get to decide how you meet them. You can ask yourself, *Why is this coming up right now?* You can explore, *What is this here to show me?* You can gently consider, *Am I ready to release this? Is there something here to learn?*

This is where words matter.

The story you tell yourself about your feelings determines whether they pass through you or stay stuck inside you. Compassionate language creates space. Curious language creates insight. Respectful language creates healing.

Self-love is not about avoiding uncomfortable emotions. It is about meeting them with maturity, clarity, and care. And when you do that, your past stops defining you and starts informing you.

Meeting Yourself with Compassion

Set aside a few quiet minutes for this exercise. You can write your responses down or simply reflect.This exercise creates change through awareness. When you recognize what is happening inside you and meet it with compassion, the emotional charge around the experience begins to dissolve. You stop carrying it forward into the present moment, and it no longer influences your decisions in the same way.

When you respond to yourself with understanding instead of criticism, the experience loses its grip. The old words tied to it no longer fit. Language like *I always mess things up, I made a huge mistake,* or *Why did I even do that?* naturally gives way to stronger, truer words such as *I was doing the best I could at the time, I learned something valuable,* and *Now, I know better.*

That shift matters. When the words change, the meaning changes. When the meaning changes, the emotional weight lifts. What once felt heavy no longer defines you or follows you forward.

Now bring to mind a feeling, memory, or experience that still surfaces from time to time. Choose something you are ready to work through.

- First, notice what is present:
    - What am I feeling right now?
    - What words am I using to describe this feeling?
    - How do those words affect how I experience it?
- Next, gently shift your language:
    - What would compassion sound like here?
    - What can I acknowledge about this experience without judgment?
    - What did I learn, or what strength did this help build in me?
- Finish by offering yourself one supportive statement, such as:
    - I handled that the best I could at the time. It's okay.
    - I am allowed to grow from my experiences. I am learning.
    - I respect myself for continuing forward. I love and accept myself.

Each time you choose words rooted in understanding rather than criticism, you strengthen self-trust. You remind yourself that you are safe to feel, safe to remember, and safe to grow. That is self-love in action. Releasing what no longer serves you is empowering.

And each time you do, you reinforce a new, supportive way of thinking that moves you forward.

"I Am Enough" Always

Genuine self-worth is something many people search for, yet it already exists within you. It does not need to be earned, proven, or validated. It is not tied to productivity, appearance, status, or meeting expectations. Self-worth is the quiet foundation you were born with. When you recognize it as yours, you experience a deeper sense of ease, belonging, and acceptance. Your value is intrinsic. It remains steady through every season of life.

Living from a sense of worth rooted in achievement can feel motivating at first, but it quickly becomes draining. When approval becomes the measure, confidence rises and falls with outcomes. Self-worth anchored in truth brings stability instead. Saying, *I am enough, even at rest,* creates a different internal experience. Worth does not fluctuate based on how much you accomplish. It is present on active days and quiet days alike. Love and belonging are available now, not postponed until some future version of yourself appears.

Your self-talk provides steadiness as you move through growth and change. Simple phrases like *I am enough* or *I am worthy of love* help you return to yourself, even when circumstances shift. These words don't need to be perfect or dramatic. Their power is in their familiarity and honesty.

When doubt appears, a few supportive words can bring you back to what matters. Rather than getting pulled into self-criticism, you can remind yourself of who you are and where you're headed.

Self-reflection supports this practice. Gently notice when your sense of worth feels distant. Once you recognize a pattern, you can intentionally choose words that reflect truth. Replace old inner dialogue with statements like *My worth is steady* or *I approve of myself and my direction.*

Visualization can deepen this experience. Imagine yourself surrounded by words such as *worthy, confident, capable, strong.* Let them settle into your body. Say quietly or aloud, *I carry my sense of worth wherever I go.* This practice reinforces what your words are already teaching you. Your positive self-talk is always available to you. *I am enough. I am enough. I am enough.* Say it. Write it. Move with it. Your worth is unconditional.

Self-Worth Visualization Ritual

Close your eyes and place one hand on your heart. Take a slow breath in. Imagine yourself feeling calm and steady, surrounded by words such as **enough, capable, loving, confident, powerful, worthy, deserving.**

Draw these into your heart with each inhale. Whisper, *"I carry my enoughness wherever I go."*

Continue breathing until your body relaxes, your shoulders soften, and you feel at peace. When you are ready, finish with a phrase that feels strong and true, such as *I can do this* or *I trust myself.*

Return to this visualization whenever you want to refocus, reset, or reconnect with yourself. Practiced regularly, this kind of self-talk becomes natural. When you begin to feel grounded in your own worth, the next step is learning how to protect that inner state from influences that quietly pull you out of alignment.

Comparison: Self-Love for the Social Media Age

Endless scrolling has become second nature. Without much thought, you move through highlights of vacations, promotions, homes, and milestones while standing in line or starting your day. Each feed offers a glimpse into lives that appear exciting, successful, or perfectly put together. When taken at face value, this constant exposure can pull attention away from your own path and momentum.

It helps to remember that social media rarely shows the full picture. What you see are curated moments, chosen angles, and selective wins. The full human experience includes effort, uncertainty, learning, and growth, even when those parts stay off screen. Recognizing this allows you to view what you see with perspective rather than comparison.

Affirmations bring your focus back to yourself in this digitally busy space. When comparison shows up, pause and remind yourself, *I am on my own timeline and that is enough.* Let those words return you to your values and direction. Another supportive anchor is, *I celebrate my journey without comparing it to anyone else's.* These statements reconnect you to your progress and help you stay grounded in what matters to you.

Creating intentional digital boundaries supports self-love. Pay attention to how different accounts make you feel. Choose to mute or unfollow anything that pulls you away from confidence or clarity. This is not avoidance. It is discernment. You deserve a digital environment that supports your growth and energy. Small choices, like setting phone-free moments in the morning or evening, help create space for presence and calm.

You can also curate your feed with intention. Follow voices that reflect diversity in age, background, body type, interests, and life experience. Seeing people who align with your values or life stage expands your sense of possibility and belonging. When your feed reflects real variety, it becomes a source of inspiration rather than comparison.

Simple digital rituals can reinforce this shift. Take time each week to review saved posts and keep only what genuinely uplifts you. Share encouragement with others who show up honestly and authentically. These small actions build connections and reinforce a healthier relationship with online spaces.

The world will always share highlights. What you choose to internalize is within your control. Returning to affirmations like *I feel good about where I am* and *I trust the progress I'm making* strengthens confidence and self-trust. When you let your worth rest in your values, your growth, and your lived experience, self-love becomes steady, grounded, and deeply personal.

Say Kind Things to Your Body

How you speak about your body reflects how you relate to yourself. Body kindness begins with words and thoughts that are respectful, supportive, and grounded in appreciation rather than judgment.

What matters is how you treat your body. Body kindness focuses on care, respect, and everyday support. It shows up in how you nourish yourself, how you move, how you rest, and how you listen to what your body needs. These choices are guided by the language you use internally. When your words are kind, your decisions naturally follow.

Your body is not something to criticize. It is the vessel that allows you to live your life. It carries you through experiences, relationships, growth, and change. Every season your body moves through, reflects life being lived, not something gone wrong.

As I've gotten older, I've noticed changes. Wrinkles. Gray hair. Tired, aching hands. And then I remember that every one of those changes represents moments I would not trade. Places I've been. Experiences I've had. This body made all of that possible. Reframing my words helped me see aging not as loss, but as evolution.

When you choose words that honor your body, your relationship with yourself shifts. Appreciation replaces criticism. Respect replaces pressure. You become more present, more accepting, and more at ease in your own skin.

Interactive Reflection: Your Body Kindness Map

Draw a simple outline of a body on paper. Inside it, list what your body allowed you to do this week. Walking, breathing deeply, hugging someone you love, creating, resting, completing tasks. Next to different areas, write a thank-you or affirmation such as, "My legs support me," or, "My body carries me through my life."

This practice reinforces a powerful truth. Your body is not here to be judged or shamed. It is here to support your life. When your words reflect that truth, self-love becomes natural and grounded.

Words to Shift Your Inner Voice

These are my go-to "I am" statements when I need to shift my mindset and come back to myself. I'm sharing them because they work. When I feel overwhelmed or stressed, it's usually a signal that fear has crept in and pulled me out of the present moment.

These words bring me back to now, which is the only place where real change can happen.

At first, the shift may feel subtle. You might simply notice your body relaxing or your thoughts slowing down. That alone matters. With practice, these statements become easier to access and more natural to believe. With practice, they help rewire old patterns, strengthen self-trust, and create lasting change from the inside out, with language that supports my growth.

I Am Statements for Self-Love and Alignment

- I am creating the life I want.
- I trust my path and the choices I am making.
- I honor my timing and allow things to unfold naturally.
- I am becoming my best self, one choice at a time.
- I am happy, healthy, and continually healing.
- I am living in abundance and openness now.
- I embrace my past, respect my present, and welcome my future.
- I am open to learning, growing, and expanding.
- I speak to myself with kindness, respect, and encouragement.
- I am grounded in who I am and confident in who I am becoming.

Words to Carry With You

"I now see how owning our story and loving ourselves through that process is the bravest thing we will ever do."

— BRENÉ BROWN

"The only person who can pull me down is myself, and I'm not going to let myself pull me down anymore."

— C. JOYBELL C.

"The most powerful relationship you will ever have is the relationship with yourself."

— STEVE MARABOLI

"You yourself, as much as anybody in the entire universe, deserve your love and affection."

— BUDDHA

"I love myself, for I am a beloved child of the universe, and the universe lovingly takes care of me now."

— LOUISE HAY

"Whatever you are doing, love yourself for doing it. Whatever you are feeling, love yourself for feeling it."

— THADDEUS GOLAS

"Find the love you seek by first finding the love within yourself. Learn to rest in that place within you that is your true home."

— SRI SRI RAVI SHANKAR

"Our entire life consists ultimately in accepting ourselves as we are."

— JEAN ANOUILH

"To accept ourselves as we are means to value our imperfections as much as our perfections."

— SANDRA BIERIG

"Believing in our hearts that who we are is enough is the key to a more satisfying and balanced life."

— ELLEN SUE STERN

CHAPTER 9

CONFIDENCE

TRUSTING YOURSELF

"The more you are willing to honor and love yourself, the greater your confidence becomes."

— LOUISE HAY

Confidence isn't about being fearless or having everything figured out. It isn't something you perform for other people. Real confidence is quieter than that. It grows from self-acceptance and unconditional love for yourself. When you truly know who you are and allow yourself to be exactly that, you stop seeking approval and reassurance outside of yourself. You trust your voice, your choices, and your timing. This kind of confidence feels calm and steady, rooted in inner safety and self-respect, and it allows you to move through life grounded in who you are.

One of the biggest truths I have learned is that change often happens in slow motion. When you are in it, it can feel like nothing is moving. It can feel like you are doing the work and still having hard days, still getting triggered, still slipping into old patterns. It can feel like you are taking tiny steps that barely count.

It can feel like watching paint dry.

But then you look back and you realize something powerful. You are not where you used to be. You are in a better place than you were. You are kinder to yourself. You are calmer. You are more at peace. You are stronger in ways you did not even notice while you were growing.

That is the beauty of hindsight. It shows you that your effort mattered. It shows you that your consistency did something. It shows you that the version of you who kept going was building confidence the whole time.

I have also learned to love growth. I love learning more all the time. I love realizing that healing is not a finish line. It is a relationship with yourself. And every time you learn something new, you gain another tool. Another perspective. Another way to support yourself through life.

There is another layer of confidence that surprised me. As I became healthier emotionally, I saw that ripple outward. My children became healthier too.

Have you ever had your child say something and you know exactly where they got it from, and you think, oh man, I need to do better? That moment can be humbling, because it shows you how much they pay attention to what we say.

And then something meaningful begins to happen as you keep doing the work with your words. You start to see it reflected back. You notice your children using similar language with themselves. You hear them talk through challenges instead of shutting down. You see them struggle and keep going, guided by the words they've learned to repeat inside their own minds. Over time, those words become beliefs, and those beliefs shape how they see themselves and move through the world. That is deeply rewarding.

And if you don't have children, this still matters. Words always travel. The way you speak to yourself influences the emotional tone around you. Friends, partners, coworkers, and even strangers pick up on the language you use about effort, setbacks, and self-worth. When you choose words that support growth and resilience, you model a different way of being. Confidence spreads this way. It gives others quiet permission to speak to themselves more kindly and to rise with you.

This is why confidence matters so much. It is not only about feeling good. It is about becoming the kind of woman who keeps going, even when it is uncomfortable. It is about becoming proof to yourself that you can change your life.

You can. And the only way you lose is if you quit. If you keep going, you will make positive changes. You will create happier patterns. You will become more grounded and more steady. One day you will look back and realize that what felt slow was still working.

That is confidence.

That is power.

That is you becoming more of who you really are.

Mirror Work: Self-Talk to Boost Self-Image

Have you truly seen yourself in the mirror, not a quick glance, but a long, honest gaze? For many women, the mirror can bring up old insecurities and familiar judgments that have followed them from childhood into adulthood. You might notice tired eyes after a long week or hear a quiet inner voice offering criticism instead of kindness. Rather than avoiding your reflection or picking it apart, what if that moment became an opportunity to build confidence?

This is the foundation of mirror work, a simple yet powerful private practice.

Popularized by Louise Hay, mirror work involves speaking affirmations aloud while looking directly at yourself. It is not about forced positivity or pretending everything feels perfect. It is about creating a kinder, more supportive relationship with yourself. When you say, "I am proud of the woman I see," or, "I accept all parts of myself, inside and out," you are not speaking to a reflection. You are speaking to your deepest beliefs. Research shows that regular mirror work can interrupt negative self-talk and support self-acceptance by pairing your words with your image, helping those messages sink in more deeply.

It is normal to feel uncomfortable or self-conscious at first. That discomfort does not mean you are doing it wrong. It means you are meeting patterns that may have been shaped by years of doubt or criticism. Shifting those patterns takes patience. Awkward or imperfect moments still count. Confidence grows through consistency.

To begin a daily mirror ritual, find a quiet space with a mirror. Stand or sit comfortably and make gentle eye contact with yourself. Notice any immediate thoughts or emotions without judging them. Choose an affirmation that fits where you are that day, such as, "My reflection shows strength and possibility," or, "I am learning to treat myself with more kindness." Speak the words out loud in a warm, honest tone. There is no need to force a smile. Let the words land naturally. Continue for one to three minutes. If self-doubt arises, acknowledge it and continue anyway. Even a quiet affirmation on a difficult day is meaningful progress.

With steady practice, you may begin to notice subtle shifts. Not only in how you see yourself, but in how you carry yourself through the world. You might stand a little taller, speak with more ease, or feel less affected by others' opinions. Your self-talk can be gentle or bold, depending on what you need at the moment. The goal is to build trust and connection with yourself, one small act at a time.

After each mirror session, take a moment to reflect. You might jot a few notes in a journal or on your phone. Ask yourself, "What did I notice or feel during today's mirror work?" Over time, resistance often softens, and affirmations that once felt distant may begin to feel natural and true.

Many women discover that mirror work quietly nurtures self-compassion. You may catch yourself smiling at your reflection after a long day or noticing a sense of resilience where criticism once lived. Hard days will still come. That is part of being human. But each moment spent meeting yourself with kindness is a courageous investment in confidence.

Once you have connected with yourself in the mirror, you are ready to take the next step. From this place of awareness and self-connection, you can begin to imagine what confidence truly looks and feels like for you. This is where visualization becomes powerful, allowing you to step into the version of yourself that already exists within you.

Visualizing the Confident Version of You

Confidence exists within you, and it grows through attention, trust, and the decision to keep moving forward. After mirror work, when you feel more connected to yourself, allow your eyes to close and take a slow breath in through your nose. Gently exhale through your mouth and let your shoulders soften. Give your body permission to settle.

Begin to imagine a confident version of you. Not a perfect version, but you as you are, grounded, steady, and self-assured. Notice how confidence feels in your body. There is calm in your breath and ease in your posture. You feel present and supported from within.

As you move through your day in this visualization, notice how you carry yourself. Your movements feel natural and unforced. You speak clearly and listen fully. The way you talk to yourself is encouraging and respectful, reinforcing trust rather than doubt.

Notice how you spend your time. Your work, interests, and daily routines feel aligned with who you are. You engage in activities that energize you and allow space for what feels nourishing and meaningful. Your free time reflects intention and enjoyment.

Notice what you are wearing. Your clothing feels comfortable, expressive, and true to you. Your choices come from self-knowledge rather than approval. You feel at ease in your body and at home in yourself.

Notice your face, your expression, your presence. There is openness here. There is self-trust. You are not rushing or proving. You are simply living your life with clarity and assurance.

Gently reflect on how this version of you makes decisions and responds to challenges. Notice how she stays connected to herself and continues forward, even when things require patience. Let this sense of confidence settle into your body and become familiar.

This confident version of you is not waiting somewhere in the future. She is already within you. Each time you choose supportive words and intentional action, you give her more space to lead. When you are ready, open your eyes and carry this feeling with you as you move through your day.

Career Confidence and Success

Workplaces can ask a lot of us to grow and stretch. Many women want to step into new roles, greater visibility, or leadership. Confidence at work is built through preparation, presence, and trusting yourself in real situations. It develops as you take action, learn, and allow yourself to grow along the way.

Confidence at work is the steadiness that comes from knowing your value and bringing it forward with clarity and intention. When you prepare thoughtfully, speak from experience, and support yourself with steady language, confidence strengthens from the inside out.

I experienced this firsthand when I returned to work after having kids. That transition asked me to reconnect with myself in new ways while balancing responsibility, confidence, and growth all at once. Later in life, I felt that same stretch when I decided to become a Certified Yoga instructor. It was something I deeply wanted, and it required me to trust myself enough to step into a new chapter. I was fifty when I made that choice, which reinforced a powerful truth: growth does not have an expiration date.

What supported me most during those moments was returning to my own words. I reminded myself, I am prepared. I bring value. I am allowed to grow into something new. I didn't wait to feel completely ready. I showed up with intention, repeated supportive language, and trusted myself to learn along the way. Those words grounded me. They helped me stay present, speak with clarity, and honor my path.

Your personal self-talk keeps you connected to your strengths when expectations, comparisons, or uncertainty arise. Before a meeting, you might quietly remind yourself, My voice belongs in this room. During conversations about growth or advancement, affirm, "I am worthy of recognition and opportunity"."My perspective is valuable, and I am capable of building something meaningful." These reminders helped you stay steady. When stepping into something new, empower yourself with, I trust myself to meet this moment.

Words for Social Confidence

Confidence doesn't live in just one part of your life. The same self-trust you build at work carries into how you connect with others. Walking into a room full of new faces, whether it's a networking event, a first date, or a group gathering, invites growth. These moments ask you to step forward, be seen, and connect. Many women experience a heightened awareness in these situations, noticing their thoughts, their body, and how they're being perceived. This doesn't mean something is wrong. It means you care, and you're stretching into connection.

Before you even speak, your inner dialogue shapes the experience. Positive self-talk helps center you before you walk in, reminding you that you belong and that your presence matters. As you prepare to enter a space where you don't yet know anyone, try reassuring yourself with, "I am welcome in every space I enter." If conversation takes a moment to warm up, return to, "My presence brings value to this interaction." These words gently shift your focus from self-monitoring to genuine engagement.

A simple breath and affirmation ritual can support social ease. Pause for a moment. Breathe in slowly through your nose for four counts, then exhale gently. As you exhale, repeat, "I am at ease with new people". Do this three times. If time allows, imagine yourself listening with interest, speaking comfortably, and exchanging energy naturally. This quiet visualization prepares your body and mind to move with confidence and openness.

Positive self-talk will also support you in the natural pauses that happen during conversation. If a question catches you off guard, return to, I am enough exactly as I am. Allow yourself to respond without rushing or overthinking. Connection grows through presence, curiosity, and authenticity.

Many women have found that simple affirmations create meaningful shifts. One woman repeated, Every space I enter is better because I'm in it, before attending a business meet-up after moving to a new city. That steady reminder helped her introduce herself to one person, which led to conversation, connection, and new opportunity. Another woman used, I am at peace with who I am, while reentering the dating world. Those words allowed her to show up honestly and comfortably, without performing or proving.

Dating, networking, and building friendships are all opportunities to practice confidence in real time. Some interactions flow easily. Others unfold more slowly. Each experience strengthens your ability to stay present and open. If comparison arises, gently return to, I bring something unique simply by being here. Let connection be the goal.

Social confidence grows through repetition, choice, and kindness toward yourself. Each time you speak, listen, or show up, you reinforce your ability to connect. Celebrate the small moments, a greeting, a shared laugh, a meaningful exchange.

Words for Authenticity

Many of us learn early that blending in feels safer, so we hide accents, interests, or family traditions. These differences can start to feel like burdens, causing us to shrink back when we would rather stand tall. But what sets you apart is not a flaw. Your individuality, including the qualities you once tried to hide, is the foundation of true confidence. When you honor your uniqueness instead of apologizing for it, you step into a personal power that no one else can replicate.

Positive self-talk will help you celebrate authenticity and reshape how you view your differences. It is natural to feel hesitant at times, especially if you have experienced exclusion connected to culture, ability, love, faith, or nontraditional choices. The right words can gently shift that experience into pride and self-respect. Try affirmations such as, "My differences are my superpower," or, "I allow my true self to shine, even when I stand out." These statements move beyond acceptance and invite confidence, visibility, and honesty.

Take a moment to reflect on times you softened an opinion, hid a passion, or adjusted your appearance to blend in. Many women recognize this pattern, whether it shows up as quieting their voice at work or staying silent about a hobby that feels different. Affirmations like, "I am proud to break the mold," give you permission to take up space as yourself rather than shrinking for comfort or approval.

To reconnect with your strengths, ask yourself, "What makes me unique, and how can I honor it today?" Write down your distinctive traits, backgrounds, or experiences and pair each one with an affirmation. "My sense of humor brings light into serious rooms." "My bilingual background gives me a rare perspective." "My neurodiversity fuels creative solutions." Return to these words often, especially when doubt arises.

I have seen women create powerful change by embracing what once made them feel different. One artist living with a rare illness used her hospital experiences as inspiration and wrote on her studio wall, "My story makes my art powerful." Her work resonated deeply with others who felt unseen. Another woman chose to wear her natural curls at work, finding both personal freedom and inspiring solidarity that eventually led to policy change. She began each morning with the affirmation, "I am enough, I love myself just as I am."

Priya, who created fusion desserts, hesitated to share her ideas at first because they felt too unconventional. When she began affirming, "My passion deserves a place at the table," she started selling at local markets. Customers loved the originality, and others felt encouraged to share their own stories and creations. Her business grew not by blending in, but by standing confidently apart.

Honoring your differences through affirmations often inspires others to do the same. Authenticity is contagious. It invites those around you to release their masks and show up more fully.

Confidence Is Already Yours

And finally, be yourself without shrinking.

I keep a quote in my car that has guided me through many moments of doubt and growth:

> ***"Stop asking for permission to be powerful. You were born powerful."***

— LISA NICHOLS

Those words are a reminder that confidence is not something you earn later. It is something that lives within you, waiting for you to trust it, listen to it, and allow it to lead.

You do not need permission to let your light shine. You are allowed to be creative, curious, playful, expressive, thoughtful, and bold. You are allowed to try new things, make mistakes, learn as you go, and evolve in ways that surprise you.

Confidence grows when you give yourself room to be human. When you stop editing yourself to fit expectations and begin honoring who you truly are. When you allow all parts of you to exist, not just the polished or productive ones. You are doing your best, and that is more than enough.

Give yourself grace as you are becoming. It unfolds through intention, patience, and the words you choose to guide yourself forward. It really is all in the words.

And every time you choose words that support you, encourage you, and remind you of your worth, you strengthen the belief that you are powerful, and exactly where you need to be.

Words to Carry With You

"As soon as you trust yourself, you will know how to live."

— JOHANN WOLFGANG VON GOETHE

"It is not the mountain we conquer, but ourselves."

— EDMUND HILLARY

"We don't see things as they are; we see them as we are."

— ANAÏS NIN

"No one can make you feel inferior without your consent."

— ELEANOR ROOSEVELT

"There is a force that controls all your decisions. It influences how you think and feel every moment you're alive. That force is your beliefs."

— TONY ROBBINS

"You are responsible for what you say and do. You are not responsible for whether or not people freak about it."

— JEN SINCERO

"I trust the next step will reveal itself when I'm ready."

— LOUISE HAY

"You may encounter many defeats, but you must not be defeated."

— MAYA ANGELOU

"Confidence comes from honoring who you are, not shrinking to fit who you think you should be."

— LISA NICHOLS

"Confidence comes not from knowing you will always succeed, but from knowing you can survive if you don't."

— BRENÉ BROWN

"Confidence is not something you have; it's something you create through action."

— MEL ROBBINS

CHAPTER 10

COURAGE

CHOOSING GROWTH

"It takes courage to grow up and become who you really are."

— E.E. CUMMINGS

Courage is the willingness to change. It is the decision to grow, to improve, and to become more than who you were yesterday. Courage is choosing a better way of being even when the old way feels familiar. It is the inner yes to personal growth, self-responsibility, and a life that feels more aligned and fulfilling.

Courage is not about fearlessness. It is about honesty. It is the courage to look at your life and say, I want more clarity. I want more peace. I want to feel better in my own skin. It is the courage to stop repeating patterns that no longer serve you and begin choosing words, thoughts, and actions that support who you are becoming.

It takes courage to be happy. It takes courage to release resistance, to think differently, and to let go of the inner struggle that keeps you stuck. It takes courage to stop arguing with yourself and start trusting yourself. Growth requires courage because it asks you to move forward without guarantees, but with intention.

Courage is also the willingness to hope again. To believe that change is possible. To trust that you can create a life that feels calmer, healthier, and more meaningful. Hope is not naïve. Hope is a brave choice. Trusting yourself and your path is a powerful act of courage.

Courage lives in the words you choose. When your inner language supports growth instead of fear, courage becomes accessible. You begin to speak honestly, set boundaries, calm your nervous system, and begin again when needed.

This chapter is about courage in real life. The courage to speak up. The courage to set boundaries. The courage to face anxiety with steadiness. The courage to begin again. It is a series of small, intentional choices that shape who you become. And every time you choose words that support truth, clarity, and growth, you strengthen your ability to live with courage.

Speaking Up and Setting Boundaries

Courage is the steady resolve to speak up even when your voice shakes. You may recognize it in moments like sharing an idea in a meeting, setting a boundary with a family member, or acknowledging that a friendship no longer supports who you are becoming. Real courage is choosing to honor yourself and speak with intention, even when it feels uncomfortable. In those moments, affirmations help you stay grounded, reminding you that your voice matters, even when doubt creeps in.

Words are powerful, especially when you use them to declare who you are and what you need. In relationships, at work, and in everyday interactions, there can be pressure to stay silent in order to avoid discomfort or conflict. But self-expression is essential. Affirming, "My voice matters and deserves to be heard," creates an internal shift. Holding this belief supports you in speaking your truth. There is strength in saying, "I express my needs clearly and kindly." These words give you permission to communicate with honesty and empathy. Repeating an affirmation in the mirror before a difficult conversation can steady your nerves and help your words land with clarity.

Setting boundaries can feel challenging at first. You may feel pressure to say yes or experience guilt when you protect your time and energy. Boundaries are not walls. They create healthier relationships with others and with yourself. Affirmations such as, "It's okay to say no without guilt," or, "I honor my needs even if others don't understand," reinforce self-respect. Picture yourself being asked to take on extra responsibilities at work. Before responding, pause, breathe, and remind yourself, "I am allowed to protect my well-being." Saying, "Thank you for thinking of me, but I need to decline so I can honor my current commitments," reflects confidence and care.

Saying no may feel uncomfortable at first. Fear of disappointing others, being judged, or losing approval can surface. This reaction is common and does not reflect weakness. Many women struggle with people-pleasing, especially if they are known for being dependable. That pattern does not define you. Self-talk such as, "I am not responsible for others' reactions to my boundaries," or, "My worth is not measured by how much I give," help separate your self-worth from external expectations. You are not required to manage everyone else's emotions. Showing up honestly and respectfully is enough.

Boundary-setting develops with practice and self-trust. Early attempts may lead you to replay conversations or question yourself. Over time, confidence grows alongside clarity. Each boundary you set strengthens your sense of self.

Mapping Your Boundaries

Find a quiet moment and write the question: "Where in my life do I need a boundary?" Answer honestly. This might involve work, family, friendships, or how you treat yourself. Choose one area and create an affirmation that supports it. For example, "I have the right to protect my peace," or, "My value is not based on how much I take on." Keep your affirmation visible and return to it whenever doubt arises.

Courage is built through daily acts of honest expression and intentional boundaries. Each time you voice your needs, even softly, you reinforce the truth that your feelings matter and your space deserves respect. They remind you that it is safe, necessary, and empowering to use your voice.

Grounding Yourself: Quick Courage

Anxiety can show up anywhere. At work, in public, or during quiet moments at home. Your body may tense, your thoughts may race, or you may feel disconnected from the present moment. These signals are not failures. They are messages asking for reassurance and grounding.

Pause and Practice

When emotions rise or uncertainty shows up, simple rituals paired with intentional words can help you return to steadiness.

- Place one hand on your heart and the other on your abdomen
- Inhale slowly through your nose for a count of four, allowing your belly to rise

- Pause briefly
- Exhale through your mouth for a count of four, letting tension soften

As you inhale, silently say, *I am safe.*
As you exhale, imagine any tightness easing.

Repeat several times, allowing your body to relax and breath to settle.

Grounding yourself physically helps bring you back into the present. Sit or stand with your feet firmly on the ground. Notice the support beneath you. Press your feet gently downward and remind yourself, "I am here. I am supported." If you are in public, keep your eyes open with a soft gaze. If you are alone, closing your eyes may deepen the effect.

Carry a small physical object that feels comforting, such as a smooth stone, bracelet, or ring. When anxiety rises, touch it and repeat, "I am steady. I am grounded." This object becomes a cue for calm, reminding your body that safety is available.

Music is another powerful grounding tool. Create a short playlist of songs that evoke strength, calm, or hope. When anxiety appears, listen intentionally and silently repeat, "Calm is possible now," or allow the music to do the work for you.

You can act while feeling uneasy. Use your self-talk to move forward such as, "I can feel anxious and still take the next step," or, "I carry calm with me," support action without resistance. When anxiety arises, meet it with steadiness rather than judgment. Pause and acknowledge, "This feels uncomfortable, and I am safe." Notice where you feel it in your body and breathe into that space. Remind yourself, "I choose how I respond."

These grounding rituals are portable and effective. Use them before important conversations, during stressful moments, or anytime you need to reconnect with yourself. Practice them even when you feel calm so they are available when you need them most.

Courage for Change

Courage to grow begins when you decide you want something different or something more for yourself. Maybe looking for a new life adventure. Growth carries wisdom. You are moving forward with experience, awareness, and strength that only comes from living. Every step you take is informed by what you've already learned about yourself.

I experienced this kind of courage when I moved to a new town and started fresh on my own. It was outside my comfort zone and required trust, adaptability, and a willingness to believe in myself in a new way. What I discovered was that courage grows each time you listen to yourself and act in alignment with who you are becoming.

Courage for change begins when something inside you starts pulling you forward. You feel ready to shift because you've grown, learned, or outgrown where you are. Sometimes it's from boredom. Sometimes it's curiosity. Sometimes it's the quiet knowing that there's more for you to explore. Even good change can feel a little scary, and that's where courage comes in.

Applying for a job. Changing a routine. Exploring a new interest. Taking a step toward health, creativity, or independence. Each one is an act of self-trust. You don't need certainty to begin. You need willingness and the courage to listen to yourself.

Courage is knowing you can learn as you go, meet new challenges, build new connections, and give yourself permission to explore what's next. Each step forward is an invitation to create a life that reflects who you are now.

Your words matter deeply during times of change. They shape how you see yourself and what you believe is possible next. Instead of replaying old narratives, you might affirm, *Every day offers a new beginning,* or *I trust myself to navigate what comes next.* These words create momentum and keep you focused on the present, where progress actually happens.

Words to Carry With You

"Courage starts with showing up and letting ourselves be seen."

— BRENÉ BROWN

"You gain strength, courage, and confidence by every experience in which you really stop to look fear in the face."

— ELEANOR ROOSEVELT

"Feel the fear and do it anyway."

— SUSAN JEFFERS

"Encouragement is the fuel on which hope runs."

— ZIG ZIGLAR

"Courage doesn't always roar. Sometimes courage is the quiet voice at the end of the day saying, 'I will try again tomorrow.'"

— MARY ANNE RADMACHER

"Trust yourself. You know more than you think you do."

— BENJAMIN SPOCK

"Your life does not get better by chance. It gets better by change."

— JIM ROHN

"And the day came when the risk to remain tight in a bud was more painful than the risk it took to blossom."

— ANAÏS NIN

CHAPTER 11

FORGIVENESS

RELEASE AND BE FREE

"When you forgive, you release yourself from the emotional prison of the past."

— BOB PROCTOR

Some days, you experience a heaviness you didn't expect, memories surfacing that you thought you had already made peace with. Even when you understand that the past cannot be changed, the sadness can still linger. Forgiveness doesn't mean the pain wasn't real. It means you're ready to stop carrying it.

There are experiences from our earlier years that shape us deeply, especially relationships that didn't feel safe, supportive, or loving. As we grow older, we may find ourselves wishing things had been different, grieving what we didn't receive. That longing can keep us tethered to the past, quietly influencing how we see ourselves and how we show up in the present. Forgiveness becomes an act of freedom when you choose to release what no longer belongs to who you are becoming.

Letting go doesn't happen all at once. It happens in layers, as you're ready. Sometimes pain resurfaces not because you're moving backward, but because you're strong enough now to release more. When this happens, you have a choice. You can shame yourself for feeling it again, or you can meet it with compassion and allow it to move through you.

For me, forgiveness often looks like release. I imagine handing the weight of old pain to a higher power, trusting that I don't have to hold it anymore. Other times, I write everything out and tear the paper apart, or release it through ritual in nature. These acts aren't about erasing the past. They are about clearing the energy attached to the words, memories, and emotions that no longer serve me.

What I've learned is this: forgiveness isn't forgetting. It's choosing freedom. It's deciding that your future matters more than the pain of what happened before. Each time you release, even a little, you reclaim energy for the life you're creating now.

If old feelings surface again, try meeting them with gratitude instead of frustration. Grateful that you are becoming aware. Grateful that you have tools. Gratitude that you no longer have to hurt. Healing doesn't mean nothing ever comes up again. It means you know how to care for yourself when it does.

This chapter is here to remind you that forgiveness is not weakness. It's strength. It's self-respect. And most of all, it's permission to be free.

Release Practice: Identifying and Letting Go

Sometimes forgiveness begins with a feeling you can't quite name. You may feel sad, angry, heavy, irritated, or disconnected, even when life appears to be going well. This doesn't mean something is wrong with you. It often means something within you is asking to be acknowledged and released.

Begin by noticing your emotional state without judging it. Ask yourself gently: What am I feeling right now? Sadness? Anger? Disappointment? Guilt? A sense of not being enough?

Sit with the feelings for a moment. Often, clarity comes when you stop telling yourself you *shouldn't* feel this way. Feeling "blah" or down is often a signal that an old belief, memory, or unmet need is surfacing.

Once you identify the feeling, ask:

- What does this feeling want me to know?
- Is there something I'm still holding onto?
- Is this connected to a memory, a belief about myself, or a relationship from the past?

You don't need perfect answers. A word, a phrase, or a single memory is enough.

Take a piece of paper and begin with whatever comes to mind. You don't need to know what you're writing about yet. Just start. A word, a sentence, a feeling — anything is enough to begin.

At first, you may feel unsure. You might think, *I don't know what to say,* or *Nothing is coming up.* That's okay. Keep writing anyway. Write that you don't know what to write. Write what you're feeling in your body. Often, the act of writing is what opens the door.

As thoughts begin to surface, let them come without judgment. Don't censor yourself. Don't correct your spelling. Don't worry about handwriting or staying in the lines. Let it be messy. Let it be honest. This isn't about fixing anything or figuring it all out. It's about allowing what's been held inside and out onto the page.

If difficult thoughts or emotions appear, resist the urge to analyze them. Just write them down. You are not here to evaluate or explain. Trust that your body and mind know what they are ready to let go of.

You'll know when you're finished. The words will slow. Nothing new will come to mind. Your hand might cramp, or you might simply feel a sense of completion. Even if it doesn't feel dramatic, something has shifted. You are releasing, whether you realize it in the moment or not.

When you're done, pause. Take a moment to appreciate yourself for showing up and making time for your well-being. This is self-care. This is self-love. And it matters. You matter. Choosing to do this is a meaningful step.

You may feel emotional afterward. That's normal. Take a few slow, steady breaths. Say your mantra. Repeat a favorite affirmation. Or do a brief visualization that brings you back to calm. Above all, allow yourself to feel whatever sense of peace or relief is present.

When you're ready, it's time to let the paper go because these are emotions you no longer need to carry. Let it go. Either way, trust that you've done the work.

Forgiveness often happens in layers. Feelings may resurface again in the future, not because you failed to heal, but because you are ready to release more. Each time you choose awareness and compassion over shame, you loosen the hold of the past and reclaim space for who you are becoming.

Forgiveness as Freedom

Forgiveness is often misunderstood as something we owe others. In truth, forgiveness is a choice we make for ourselves. It is not about excusing harm, minimizing pain, or forgetting what happened. It is about releasing the emotional weight of the past so it no longer shapes how we feel, think, and respond in the present.

Forgiveness allows you to acknowledge real pain without living inside it. Some experiences, especially those involving different forms of abuse, leave deep imprints on the body and nervous system. Letting go is not simple, and it is never forced. Forgiveness unfolds in ways that feel safe, personal, and embodied. It often happens slowly, in layers, and only when you are ready.

Choosing forgiveness is choosing freedom. It is deciding that past experiences no longer influence your present-day choices or limit who you are becoming. When old wounds remain unresolved, they can surface as sadness, anger, self-doubt, or patterns that quietly work against you. Letting go is not about what others deserve. It is about what *you* deserve.

You cannot change what happened, but you can change how it lives in you now. Each time you reframe a thought, release stored emotion, or choose compassion over self-blame, you are training your mind and nervous system to support your healing. This is how forgiveness becomes an act of self-respect. It creates space for clarity, peace, and growth that supports the life you are building.

Visualization: Returning to Yourself

Close your eyes or soften your gaze.

Imagine yourself resting on a blanket beneath a tree. The ground beneath you feels steady and supportive. The sun is shining, and the temperature is just right — warm, comfortable, and soothing. A gentle breeze moves through the leaves above you, and everything around you feels calm and peaceful.

Notice how safe you feel here. Your body is relaxed. Your breath is easy. You are exactly where you are meant to be. There is no rush. You have all the time you need.

As you rest, imagine looking at yourself with love, compassion, and understanding. See yourself as you are in this moment, and allow appreciation to arise for who you are and how far you've come. Feel kindness toward yourself. Feel acceptance. Let yourself be held in that feeling.

In this peaceful space, begin to imagine what you want to create in your life. Not from pressure, but from clarity and self-trust. You are in the right place at the right time. Picture yourself living in a way that feels aligned, meaningful, and fulfilling. Notice how your body responds as you allow yourself to believe this is possible.

Take a slow breath in and gently remind yourself:

I have the power to shift.

With each breath, feel that knowing settle deeper. When you see this life and allow yourself to believe in it, your body softens. You feel calm. You feel steady. You feel supported.

You feel grateful for the life you have. You have created a happy, fulfilling life, and you are allowing all that is in store for you. This sense of gratitude expands in your chest, creating space for joy, ease, and possibility.

When you're ready, gently return your attention to the present moment, carrying this feeling of peace, self-love, and abundance with you.

Giving Yourself Grace

Regret and guilt often come from the way we speak to ourselves. The *should have, would have, could have* thoughts replay old moments and keep shame alive. Even when we understand that we were doing the best we could at the time, negative self-talk can pull us back into blaming ourselves for what we didn't know or couldn't see then.

This is where grace becomes essential.

Giving yourself grace means recognizing your humanity. It means allowing room for mistakes, growth, and learning without turning them into proof that you are flawed or unworthy. Grace softens the inner dialogue. It interrupts the cycle of shame and replaces it with understanding.

In words, grace sounds like kindness. It sounds like, "I did the best I could with what I knew." It sounds like, "I am allowed to learn." It sounds like, "I don't have to keep reliving this to grow." Grace changes the language you use with yourself so that your inner world becomes a place of support. In action, grace looks like patience. It looks like pausing when self-criticism arises and choosing not to pile on. It looks like allowing yourself to rest, to feel, and to heal at your own pace. Grace is choosing to be patient with your process.

When you offer yourself grace, you loosen the grip of regret and create space for forgiveness to take hold. Each time you choose grace over self-blame, you quiet the past and strengthen the present. This is how forgiveness becomes sustainable. This is how healing continues.

Grace Affirmations

- I give myself grace as I learn and grow.
- I did the best I could with what I knew at the time.
- I release the need to punish myself for being human.
- I allow myself to learn without shame.
- I am gentle with myself as I heal.
- I choose compassion over self-criticism.
- I do not need to relive the past to grow from it.
- I am allowed to move forward with understanding and kindness.
- I offer myself patience as I become who I am meant to be.
- I let grace guide my thoughts, my words, and my healing.

Words That Set You Free

This is why words matter. Sometimes a few simple sentences can soften something that's been held tightly for years. They arrive exactly when you need them, offering relief, perspective, and permission to let go.

Forgiveness is giving up the hope that the past could have been any different.
Forgiveness begins when we stop punishing ourselves for being human.
You don't forgive to forget. You forgive to be free.

Let these words settle. Feel what shifts as you read them. Forgiveness doesn't erase what happened, but it releases the grip those experiences have on you now. It loosens the weight. It opens space. It reminds you that healing is possible, and that you don't have to carry everything forever.

If you're feeling lighter, more open, or simply a little more at ease, trust that. That's your nervous system responding to compassion and truth. This is self-love. This is empowerment. This is what happens when you choose words that support your becoming.

Words to Carry With You

"Forgiveness is not an occasional act, it is a constant attitude."

— MAYA ANGELOU

"Forgiveness is a gift you give yourself."

— SUZANNE SOMERS

"Forgiveness does not change the past, but it does enlarge the future."

— PAUL BOESE

"Letting go doesn't mean forgetting. It means you stop carrying the energy of the past into the present."

— BRENÉ BROWN

"Forgiveness is about freeing yourself, not about letting someone else off the hook."

— TONY ROBBINS

"You don't move on by pretending nothing happened. You move on by deciding it no longer controls you."

— MEL ROBBINS

"Grace means that all of your mistakes now serve a purpose instead of serving shame."

— ANNE LAMOTT

"Forgiveness is choosing to live without resentment, even when you remember."

— JACK CANFIELD

"Forgiveness means letting go of the past."

— GERALD G. JAMPOLSKY

"Grace finds us where we are, but it does not leave us where it found us."

— ANNE LAMOTT

CHAPTER 12

GRATITUDE

SEEING YOUR GROWTH

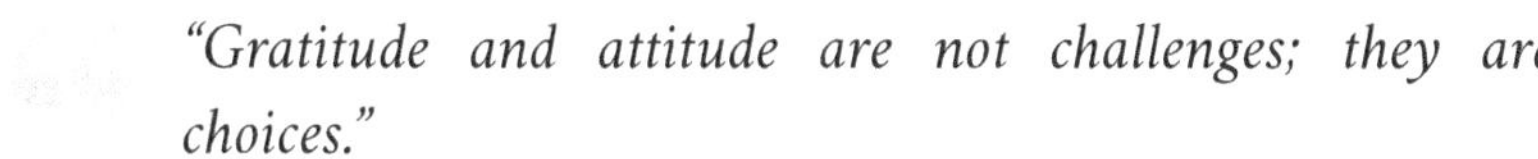

"Gratitude and attitude are not challenges; they are choices."

— ROBERT BRAATHE

Gratitude as Recognition

Gratitude is often spoken about as something polite or expected. Something you're supposed to practice because it sounds good or makes you seem positive. But real gratitude is far deeper than that. It is not forced optimism or pretending everything is perfect. Gratitude, at its core, is awareness.

It is the moment you pause and truly see yourself.

Gratitude means recognizing how far you've come. Noticing the ways you think differently now. Seeing the small shifts in how you respond, how you speak to yourself, how you move through your day. It is appreciating who you are becoming, not just what you have.

This kind of gratitude is powerful because it changes perspective. When you begin to notice your growth, you stop measuring yourself only by what still feels unfinished. You start to recognize progress instead of pressure. Effort instead of expectation. Learning instead of judgment.

Gratitude helps you see yourself differently.

Courage asks you to try. To speak up. To keep going even when growth feels uncomfortable. Gratitude allows you to step back and say, *Wow, look at what I'm learning. Look at how I'm changing.* That recognition builds confidence, steadiness, and trust in your own process.

Gratitude grounds you in the present moment. And the present moment is where your power lives. When you're present, you're not stuck replaying the past or worrying about what comes next. You are here, aware, and able to choose how you respond.

Practicing gratitude is about honoring the work you are doing. Choosing a new way of thinking, speaking, and living takes courage and intention. It is brave. It is intentional. When you recognize your growth, you reinforce it. Gratitude becomes a practice of seeing clearly and responding with respect.

This chapter is an invitation to slow down and notice the ways you are already changing your life, one word, thought and choice at a time. That awareness is gratitude in action.

The One-Breath Gratitude Reset

A single mindful breath can shift your entire day. Whether you are in your kitchen between tasks, sitting in your car, or just finishing a conversation, you can pause and return to the present moment. In that pause, gratitude becomes available. The one-breath gratitude reset is a simple, practical tool that brings you back to awareness with just one intentional breath.

This practice works because it fits into real life. It does not require silence, solitude, or extra time. Simply pause, inhale deeply, and name one thing you are grateful for. It can be something small and ordinary, like sunlight through a window, a favorite beverage, a completed task, a supportive text, or comfortable pajamas. As you exhale, pair the breath with a supportive statement such as, "I am grateful for this moment," or, "Thank you, body, for carrying me today." Your breath grounds you, and gratitude gives that moment meaning.

You can also gently guide the breath with simple language. Inhale with the word gratitude. Exhale with the word release. This pattern helps you re-center, even when your day feels full or fast.

This brief practice does make a difference. Regular moments of gratitude support emotional balance, improve mood, and help your nervous system settle. When gratitude is paired with breath, something you already do all day long, it becomes natural and accessible. Noticing things to appreciate requires less effort and begins to happen automatically.

Affirmations you can use with your one-breath reset:

- I am grateful for being me.
- I am grateful for learning new things.
- I appreciate the small joys right now.
- I am grateful for the sun, nature, and the world I live in.
- Inhale positivity. Exhale negativity. .
- I am grateful for life experiences.

Use one whenever it feels right. While your computer loads, while standing in line, before starting your car, or between tasks. This is easy to become a part of your daily rhythm.

You can also weave the one-breath reset into transitions. Before checking your inbox, pause and feel gratitude for stability. After a meal, acknowledge nourishment. As you move from work to home, from one red light to the next, let one breath mark the shift.

A few of these resets throughout your day can ease anxiety, increase patience, and help you notice beauty more easily. If you want to observe the impact, keep a simple gratitude journal or mental tally. After a few days, reflect on how your mood feels and what you are noticing more often. The goal is awareness. Even one grateful breath has the power to change how you experience the moment you are in.

Affirmations for Finding Light on Dark Days

Some days feel heavier than others. They may carry loss, uncertainty, fatigue, or emotional weight. On those days, gratitude is not about pretending everything feels fine. It is about noticing something small that offers steadiness. A warm blanket, gentle rain, a familiar sound, a quiet moment. Gratitude and sorrow are allowed to exist together, and when they do, a thread of hope begins to form.

When gratitude feels distant, return to what is simple and real. Think of moments when life felt strained and what helped you get through. A kind message, a pet resting beside you, the comfort of your favorite blanket, a candle flickering with a familiar scent. You can gently say to yourself, "It's okay to feel heavy and still notice what supports me." This does not dismiss sadness. It allows comfort to sit beside it.

During times of illness, exhaustion, caregiving, or emotional overwhelm, gratitude becomes a stabilizing force. Try affirmations such as, "I am grateful for the support I have right now," or, "I acknowledge my pain and my resilience." Even saying, "In this moment, I notice one thing that helps," can soften the weight you are carrying.

There are moments when gratitude shows up quietly. A new mother finds five peaceful minutes alone in the shower. A woman facing illness noticing flowers blooming outside or laughter in the next room. These small recognitions do not erase difficulty, but they offer pause and breath. They remind you that even now, something supportive exists.

Gratitude does not require waiting for easier days. Often, it deepens during a challenge. When things feel dark, look for small glimmers and name them honestly. Affirmations such as, "I am grateful for the small comforts that help me through," or, "I honor my strength by noticing what remains," can be whispered or written down.

On harder days, it can help to return to a few steady constants. A safe place to rest. Clean sheets. A favorite song. Warm tea. Fresh air. A supportive person you trust. Writing these down can make them easier to reach when feeling off balance. Gratitude can coexist with every emotion. You are allowed to feel sad and grateful, tired and appreciative, all at the same time.

Gratitude does not remove the shadows. It allows light to filter in. And choosing to notice that light, is an act of courage and care for yourself.

Gratitude for Growth

It is easy to overlook your progress when you measure yourself against an ideal. Perfection pulls your attention away from the small, meaningful steps that actually create change. Gratitude shifts your focus back to what is real and unfolding. It allows you to recognize each part of your journey, even the parts that feel slow or unfinished. You can remind yourself, "I am grateful for the steps I am taking, not just where I am going." Every effort counts.

Sometimes growth is hard to see. That's why it helps to look for it in small, intentional moments. Maybe you spoke up when it felt uncomfortable, tried a new approach, or set a boundary you had been avoiding. These moments may seem small, but they reflect real inner movement. Gratitude helps you notice them. On days when progress feels invisible, affirm, "I appreciate my willingness to keep showing up," or, "I am grateful for what I am learning along the way." Persistence is the foundation of growth.

Real change most often appears as subtle shifts. You respond with more patience. You soften your inner voice. You choose rest instead of pushing. These choices matter. They signal alignment and self-respect. Growth lives in these moments.

Think of someone learning to set boundaries. At first, saying no feels awkward. Each attempt builds confidence, regardless of how smooth it feels. Over time, self-trust grows not because the process is perfect, but because it is practiced. A simple reminder like, "Every effort moves me forward," reinforces that truth.

To support this mindset, set aside time each week or month to reflect on growth. This is not about listing achievements. It is about noticing where you stretched, adapted, or handled something differently. Ask yourself, "What did I navigate better recently?" or, "How did I support myself today?" These reflections bring awareness to progress and that is something to be grateful for.

Getting through a difficult day. Trying again after disappointment. Choosing kindness toward yourself. Gratitude honors these moments too. They are evidence of resilience and inner strength.

When gratitude is rooted in growth, confidence deepens naturally. You begin to trust yourself because you see yourself evolving. Each step becomes proof that you are learning, adjusting, and committed to your own well-being.

Sharing Your Thankfulness to Uplift Others

Gratitude doesn't stop with you. When spoken out loud, it moves outward and has the power to lift the people around you. A sincere expression of appreciation can shift a moment, a relationship, or even someone's entire day. A simple "I'm grateful for you" can land more deeply than any grand gesture, especially when someone has been giving quietly or feeling unseen.

Sharing gratitude strengthens connection. It builds trust, softens tension, and creates a sense of belonging. Whether at home, at work, or with friends, expressing appreciation reminds people that they matter. Words like "Thank you for being there," or "Your support meant more than you know," affirm value and create warmth for both the giver and the receiver.

Bringing gratitude into your relationships can be simple. Start small. Send a short text, write a quick note, or say thank you out loud when someone shows up for you. One sentence is enough. "I appreciate you." "You made a difference for me today." These moments of recognition accumulate and strengthen bonds over time.

If verbal gratitude feels uncomfortable at first, create gentle rituals. A gratitude jar at home or work invites everyone to participate. Leaving kind notes, sharing affirmations, or expressing appreciation in writing allows gratitude to flow in ways that feel natural to you. These small practices create lasting reminders of care and encouragement.

Gratitude creates a ripple effect. When people feel valued, they are more likely to pass that feeling forward. Relationships grow stronger. Communities feel more connected. Even brief moments of appreciation can elevate the energy of a space and foster a sense of mutual support.

You may also notice how expressing gratitude changes you. After sharing appreciation, pause and observe. Do you feel lighter, calmer, more connected? Gratitude strengthens your awareness of support and reminds you that you are not navigating life alone.

To keep this practice alive, consider choosing a few people each week to thank intentionally. It might be a friend, a family member, a coworker, or someone who offered encouragement when you needed it. Decide how you want to express your appreciation, then notice how it affects your relationships and your sense of connection.

Sincerity is what matters most. Simple words like "Thank you for listening," "I appreciate your effort," or "You inspire me," carry real power.

As gratitude extends outward, it strengthens your inner foundation as well. It reinforces connection, uplifts others, and reminds you of the positive impact you have in the world. When gratitude is shared freely, it becomes a force that supports growth, courage, and meaningful change for everyone involved.

Thinking Thankfully

Gratitude is always a choice. You choose where your attention goes, what you name as meaningful, and how you interpret your experiences. When you practice gratitude, you shift from reacting to life to recognizing it.

I once heard that it is impossible to feel unhappy while you are being grateful. Even when difficult emotions are present, gratitude has a way of softening them. It creates space. It reminds you that alongside what is hard, there is also support. A breath. A lesson. A strength you didn't know you had. A reminder that you are still here and still growing.

Gratitude does not ask you to deny challenges. It invites you to notice what is steady and supportive at the same time. When you begin to look for moments of appreciation, even small ones, your perspective shifts. You start to see progress instead of only problems. Growth instead of only effort. You begin to recognize who you are becoming.

There is no single right way to practice gratitude. Create a way of thinking thankfully that works for you. Through breath, words, journaling, quiet reflection, or simple acknowledgments throughout your day. What matters is that it feels genuine and supportive.

Gratitude brings you back into the present moment, and the present moment is where your power lives. It is where clarity forms. It is where change happens. It is where you remember that you are capable, resilient, and moving forward.

As you continue on this path, let gratitude be a steady companion. Not as a rule, but as a reminder of how far you've come, what you've learned, and the life you are actively creating.

Words to Carry With You

"Gratitude is one of the sweet shortcuts to finding peace of mind and happiness inside. No matter what is going on outside of us, there's always something we could be grateful for."

— BARRY NEIL KAUFMAN

"My day begins and ends with gratitude."

— LOUISE HAY

"Gratitude brings me back to the present moment. I appreciate who I am and where I am right now."

— LOUISE HAY

"The more grateful I am, the more beauty I see."

— LOUISE HAY

"Gratitude unlocks the fullness of life. It turns what we have into enough, and more."

— MELODY BEATTIE

"Gratitude for the present moment and the fullness of life now is the true prosperity."

— ECKHART TOLLE

"Wear gratitude like a cloak, and it will feed every corner of your life."

— RUMI

"The miracle of gratitude is that it shifts your perception to such an extent that it changes the world you see."

— DR. ROBERT HOLDEN

"Gratitude unlocks all that's blocking us from really feeling truthful, really feeling authentic, and really feeling happy."

— GABRIELLE BERNSTEIN

"Affirmations take our thoughts to a more protective and powerful place. By affirming good, by affirming daily gratitude, you will find more peace by giving your thoughts a break from the worry cycle."

— MACHEL SHULL

"Learn everything you can, anytime you can, from anyone you can. There will always come a time when you will be grateful you did."

— SARAH CALDWELL

CONCLUSION

If you're holding these pages right now, pause for a moment and take a deep breath. Let yourself feel good about this choice. You did something meaningful. You chose to explore the power of your own words. You gave yourself space to reflect, to question old patterns, and to try something new. This kind of choice creates real change, one day and one word at a time.

Throughout this book, you've explored a simple but powerful truth. Words are building blocks. You learned how self-talk influences your thoughts, emotions, and decisions. You explored how intentional language creates new, supportive patterns. You practiced noticing old habits and gently replacing them with words that build clarity, confidence, and self-trust.

Chapter by chapter, you gathered tools for real life. On heavy days, you found words that helped steady your emotions. When motivation wavered, you learned how small shifts create momentum. Determination showed up not as perfection, but as the willingness to show up for yourself again and again. Courage invited you to speak honestly, set boundaries, and trust yourself enough to begin again.

You explored self-love and self-worth with openness, learning that kindness toward yourself is a daily practice. Confidence grew as you honored who you are. Gratitude helped you recognize your growth and ground yourself in the present moment. And through it all, you learned that empowerment begins with the language you choose.

Look at what you now hold. You know how to work with your thoughts instead of against them. You can recognize comparison, soften self-criticism, and turn setbacks into learning moments. You've practiced rituals that fit real life. You understand that change grows through awareness, intention, and consistency.

Here is what matters most. Progress counts. If you've tried even one affirmation, paused for one grateful breath, or caught yourself choosing a more supportive thought, you are moving forward. Let that matter. Celebrate it.

Thank you for trusting this process and for showing up for yourself. It takes courage to believe in your ability to grow and to speak to yourself with kindness. That courage is the heart of this work.

You hold more influence over your inner world than you may have ever realized. When you choose words with intention, you shape your life with passion, move forward with purpose, and step fully into your power. Build from your wisdom. Trust your experience. **Start speaking your power.** Let it guide how you think, how you choose, and how you show up.

This is your life. Go live it.

With love and support,

- Audrey

Let's Keep in Touch

At Pepperworks Publishing, everything we create is rooted in self-care, personal growth, natural wellness, and emotional well-being. On Instagram and Facebook, you'll find empowering and thoughtful content designed to support real life—growth, healing, curiosity, and becoming more of who you are.

It's a space for reflection, learning, and inspiration, along with gentle glimpses into the books and practices created through Pepperworks Publishing. If you enjoy words that uplift, ideas that invite you to pause and reflect, and content that supports your well-being in a grounded, approachable way, I'd love for you to join us there.

You're always welcome to connect with us on Instagram and Facebook at **@pepperworkspublishing**.

YOUR WORDS MATTER

If the words in this book have been enlightening or empowering, and reminded you that you matter, I would be truly grateful if you shared your experience in a review. Your words may help someone else discover the same sense of clarity, encouragement, and self-worth.

As an independent author, your feedback and reviews are the heartbeat of my work. They allow this book to reach others who are looking for support and personal growth.

Thank you for being here.

— Audrey Daric

WORDS TOO POWERFUL NOT TO SHARE

Some words stay with us.

They land softly, then echo for years.

These are the quotes I've gathered over time that continue to remind me what's possible, what matters, and who we are becoming.

Read them slowly. Return to them often. Let the ones that resonate meet you where you are.

"Living a life that you love and loving the life that you are living is the truest demonstration of abundance."

— LISA NICHOLS

"The purpose of our lives is to give birth to the best which is within us."

— MARIANNE WILLIAMSON

"Success is an inside job. It's not about what you do, it's about who you become."

— MARIE FORLEO

"Your problem isn't the problem. Your reaction is the problem. It's your thoughts about the problem that are causing your anxiety."

— MEL ROBBINS

"At the bottom of every one of your fears is simply the fear that you can't handle whatever life may bring you."

— SUSAN JEFFERS

"The only way to get rid of the fear of doing something is to go out and do it."

— SUSAN JEFFERS

"I am in the right place at the right time, doing the right thing."

— LOUISE HAY

"You are worthy just because you exist."

— LOUISE HAY

"Things don't happen to you, but for you."

— LOUISE HAY

"Nothing is impossible. The word itself says 'I'm possible.'"

— AUDREY HEPBURN

"Believing in our hearts that who we are is enough is the key to a more satisfying and balanced life."

— ELLEN SUE STERN

"Life isn't about finding yourself. Life is about creating yourself."

— GEORGE BERNARD SHAW

"Instead of worrying about what you cannot control, shift your energy to what you can create."

— ROY T. BENNETT

"No one can make you feel inferior without your consent."

— ELEANOR ROOSEVELT

"The pen that writes your life story must be held in your own hand."

— IRENE C. KASSORLA

"You only live once, but if you do it right, once is enough."

— MAE WEST

"Dwell in possibility."

— EMILY DICKINSON

"Happiness is not something you postpone for the future; it is something you design for the present."

— JIM ROHN

"Life is like riding a bicycle. To keep your balance, you must keep moving."

— ALBERT EINSTEIN

"It is our choices that show what we truly are, far more than our abilities."

— J.K. ROWLING

"Watch your thoughts, they become words; watch your words, they become actions; watch your actions, they become your destiny."

— LAO TZU

ABOUT THE AUTHOR

Audrey Daric is an author, lifelong learner, and passionate believer in the power of words to shape how we feel, think, and live. She is an avid reader who loves books, ideas, and exploring new ways to grow emotionally, mentally, and spiritually. Her writing is grounded, compassionate, and rooted in real life experience.

Audrey's work is inspired by her own journey of personal growth, self-discovery, and mindset shifts. Over the years, she has learned firsthand how changing the way we speak to ourselves can transform confidence, relationships, and the courage to begin again. Her books are written to feel supportive, encouraging, and practical, offering tools readers can return to whenever they need grounding, clarity, or reassurance.

When she's not writing, Audrey finds joy in kayaking, hiking, yoga, and watching sunsets. Her favorite moments are spent with her adult children, who continue to inspire her growth, curiosity, and gratitude for life. She believes deeply that being yourself is a superpower to embrace.

Audrey has written multiple books across themes of personal growth, emotional healing, and self-care. While some of her work is especially supportive for women, her writing is meant to resonate with anyone seeking growth, self-awareness, and a more intentional way of living.

Through her words, Audrey hopes to remind readers that they already carry wisdom, strength, and possibility within them. The words they choose can bring it to life.

REFERENCES

Your powerful, changeable mindset - Stanford Report https://news.stanford.edu/stories/2021/09/mindsets-clearing-lens-life

Self-affirmation activates brain systems associated with ... https://pmc.ncbi.nlm.nih.gov/articles/PMC4814782/

What Is Manifestation? Science-Based Ways to Manifest https://www.psychologytoday.com/ca/blog/click-here-for-happiness/202009/what-is-manifestation-science-based-ways-to-manifest

Negative self-talk: 8 ways to quiet your inner critic https://www.calm.com/blog/negative-self-talk

99 Positive Morning Affirmations You Can Use Daily https://www.thegoodtrade.com/features/positive-affirmations-morning-routine/

The 5 Triggers That Make New Habits Stick https://jamesclear.com/habit-triggers

30 Affirmations To Stop Comparing And Celebrate You https://www.thecoffeybreak.com/blog-2/2018/10/2/30-affirmations-to-stop-comparing-and-celebrate-you

31 Days Of Love: A Month Of Self-love Affirmations https://lifebydeanna.com/31-days-of-love-a-month-of-self-love-affirmations/

The Power of Positive Affirmations | Old Dominion University https://www.odu.edu/equity/civility-month/affirmations

Positive Affirmations for Anxiety Relief | The Best Affirmations https://cogbtherapy.com/cbt-blog/positive-affirmations-for-anxiety-relief

Inspirational Social Media Quotes to Share with Your ... https://socialtradia.com/blog/inspirational-social-media-quotes/

The Power of Gratitude and How Busy Women can use it ... https://www.eatsleepyoga.net/blog/the-power-of-gratitude-amp-how-busy-women-can-use-it-as-self-care

Inspirational Quotes From Women of Color | Ellevate https://www.ellevatenetwork.com/articles/7994-inspirational-quotes-from-women-of-color

Moving Stories of Real People in Affirmation https://affirmation.org/affirmation-stories/

Embrace Change and New Beginnings: Affirmations for a ... https://yvelettestines.com/f/embrace-change-and-new-beginnings-affirmations-for-a-fresh-start

From Vision Board to Reality: Success Stories from Real ... https://medium.com/@sadraxta/from-vision-board-to-reality-success-stories-from-real-people-d1cc6c1d870d

The Power of Small Wins https://hbr.org/2011/05/the-power-of-small-wins

22 Simple Affirmations for a Midweek Energy Boost https://www.affirmations.online/22-simple-affirmations-for-a-midweek-energy-boost/

50 Quotes About Resilience from Women—Mostly https://www.inhersight.com/blog/insight-commentary/quotes-about-resilience

60+ Positive Affirmations for Women https://www.morelandobgyn.com/blog/positive-affirmations-for-women

25 Empowering Quotes Celebrating Women's Strength and ... https://www.embracerelief.org/25-empowering-quotes-celebrating-womens-strength-and-resilience/

44 Powerful Affirmations to Overcome Limiting Beliefs https://www.affirmations.online/44-powerful-affirmations-to-overcome-limiting-beliefs/

9 Women in Tech Share Their Stories About Imposter ... https://builtin.com/articles/9-women-tech-share-their-stories-about-imposter-syndrome

Why Celebrating Small Wins Boosts Motivation (The Science) https://www.upskillist.com/blog/why-celebrating-small-wins-boosts-motivation/

37 Affirmations for Setting Boundaries https://lovingmywild.com/affirmations-for-setting-boundaries/

Real World Examples of Overcoming Self Doubt https://www.linkedin.com/pulse/real-world-examples-overcoming-self-doubt-james-career-coach

10+ Mindful Grounding Techniques (Incl. Group Exercise) https://positivepsychology.com/grounding-techniques/

100 Uplifting Quotes About New Beginnings | SUCCESS https://www.success.com/95-uplifting-quotes-about-new-beginnings/

100+ Forgiveness Affirmations For Freedom, Healing & Peace https://blog.gratefulness.me/forgiveness-affirmations/

Self-Compassion Practices: Cultivate Inner Peace and Joy https://self-compassion.org/self-compassion-practices/

Rituals to Release Resentment and Find Peace https://originalbotanica.com/blog/rituals-to-release-resentment-and-find-peace

Forgiveness and Letting Go Quotations - School of Social Work https://socialwork.buffalo.edu/resources/self-care-starter-kit/additional-self-care-resources/inspirational-materials/forgiveness-and-letting-go-quotations.html

What is Mirror Work? https://www.louisehay.com/what-is-mirror-work/

4 Confidence Affirmations For Ambitious Women In ... https://heragenda.com/p/confidence-affirmations-womens-history-month-women-leadership/

5 Affirmations to Overcome Social Anxiety https://www.psychologytoday.com/us/blog/platonic-love/202404/5-affirmations-to-overcome-social-anxiety

Quotes From 25 Famous Women on Self-Expression https://www.thecut.com/2017/08/quotes-from-25-famous-women-on-self-expression.html

The Effect of Body-Focused Positive Psychology ... https://link.springer.com/article/10.1007/s41042-023-00134-1

Beyond Body Positive: Affirmations for Healing Body Image https://www.rootedrecoveryrd.com/blog/body-positive-affirmations

Changes in Women's Self-Esteem in the Social Media Age https://www.psichi.org/blogpost/987366/505432/From-Instagram-to-TikTok-Changes-in-Women-s-Self-Esteem-in-the-Social-Media-Age

Success Stories https://freeaffirmations.org/success-stories

Gratitude enhances health, brings happiness — and may ... https://www.health.harvard.edu/blog/gratitude-enhances-health-brings-happiness-and-may-even-lengthen-lives-202409113071

Take a Gratitude Breath https://tinkergarten.com/activities/take-a-gratitude-breath

50 Fearless Gratitude Affirmations to Start Using Today https://fearlessliving.org/fearless-gratitude-affirmations

Overcoming Adversity: The Power of Gratitude ~ by Katelyn https://www.nerdygirlsuccess.com/overcoming-adversity-the-power-of-gratitude/

Empowering Affirmations for Women to Boost Self-Esteem https://www.mentalhealth.com/tools/200-daily-positive-affirmations-for-women

The difference between a goal and an intention. https://www.holstee.com/blogs/mindful-matter/the-difference-between-a-goal-and-an-intention

Unbelievable Manifestation!! - The Secret® Stories https://www.thesecret.tv/stories/unbelievable-manifestation/

10 Effective Methods for Tracking and Measuring Personal ... https://gritdaily.com/tracking-and-measuring-personal-development-progress/